CULTURES OF THE WORLD®

NEW ZEALAND

Roselynn Smelt & Yong Jui Lin

Marshall Cavendish
Benchmark
New York

PICTURE CREDITS

Cover photo: © Jon Arnold / Danita Delimont Stock Photograph

alt.TYPE / REUTERS: 81, 107, 111 • ANA Press Agency: 48 • Corbis: 31, 60, 62, 79, 83, 94, 104, 110, 126 • David Simson: 11, 23, 24, 33, 34, 41, 43, 68, 84, 95, 96 • Focus Team Italy: 13, 14 • Getty Images: 26, 27, 37, 51, 71, 87, 99, 106, 109, 112 • Hutchison Library: 7, 65, 67 • Lonely Planet Images: 1, 5, 6, 8, 10, 12, 15, 18, 30, 38, 39, 40, 46, 49, 52, 53, 57, 63, 72, 76, 88, 90, 92, 97, 105, 116, 123, 128 • Murray Ball: 80 • Nik Wheeler: 101 • North Wind Picture Archives: 21 • Photolibrary: 17, 32, 50, 54, 58, 59, 78, 82, 91, 98, 100, 102, 108, 113, 114, 115, 122, 124, 125, 127, 129, 130, 131 • Susanna Burton: 4, 16, 22, 45, 47, 64, 69, 70, 73, 74, 85, 117, 118, 119, 120 • TopFoto: 3, 9, 19, 20, 25, 42, 44, 75

PRECEDING PAGE

Maori woman doing a traditional dance in Roturua.

Publisher (U.S.): Michelle Bisson
Editors: Deborah Grahame, Mindy Pang
Copyreader: Tara Koellhoffer
Designer: Benson Tan
Cover picture researcher: Connie Gardner
Picture researcher: Thomas Khoo

Marshall Cavendish Benchmark
99 White Plains Road
Tarrytown, NY 10591
Web site: www.marshallcavendish.us

Library of Congress Cataloging-in-Publication Data
Smelt, Roselynn,
   New Zealand : by Roselynn Smelt & Yong Jui Lin. — 2nd ed.
     p. cm. — (Cultures of the world)
   Summary: "Provides comprehensive information on the geography, history, wildlife, governmental structure, economy, cultural diversity, peoples, religion, and culture of New Zealand"—Provided by publisher.
   Includes bibliographical references and index.
   ISBN 978-0-7614-3415-3
   1. New Zealand—Juvenile literature. I. Yong, Jui Lin. II. Title.
DU408.S56 2009
993—dc22   2008028792

Printed in China
7 6 5 4 3 2 1

CONTENTS

A Maori carving found in a meeting house in Waitangi.

A happy hedge in the town of Tauranga on the North Island.

INTRODUCTION

THE LAND OF NEW ZEALAND has shaped its people, as the people have struggled to shape the land. The nation's two main cultures—Maori and Pakeha—are as distinct as the forested mountains are from the crystal clear lakes and roaring rivers, but they are also united—and divided—by the rugged land they have conquered and tamed.

The Maori (MAA-or-i, an ethnic minority living in New Zealand) and Pakeha (PAA-ke-haa, white New Zealanders) are working together to settle the remaining land claims that are arising out of the legacy left to them by the British colonizers and the Treaty of Waitangi that was signed in 1840. As old wounds are healed, New Zealand is becoming a nation that is more at peace with itself. Long free of its colonial ties to Great Britain, New Zealand has emerged as a confident and significant player on the world stage. This book in the *Cultures of the World* series takes a look at the important aspects of New Zealand life that help define its identity as a dynamic, independent, young nation.

GEOGRAPHY

NEW ZEALAND, which consists of the North and South Islands and several smaller islands, most notably Stewart Island/Rakiura and the Chatham Islands, lies about 1,250 miles (2,000 km) southeast of Australia and 1,400 miles (2,250 km) north of Antarctica.

With a total land area of 103,738 square miles (268,680 square km), the country is about the size of the state of Colorado. Stretching over 1,000 miles (1,600 km) from north to south and some 280 miles (450 km) across, the slim islands of New Zealand exhibit an amazing diversity of scenery and an impressively long coastline.

Between the subtropical waters of the north and the sub-Antarctic ocean of the south, there are about 9,404 miles (15,134 km) of coastline. Spectacular harbors are found in the often-indented and unspoiled coastline, which is more than half the coastal length of the United States. The two main islands, North and South, are separated by the Cook Strait, which is about 19 miles (30 km) wide at its narrowest point.

Because they are close to the international dateline (an imaginary line on the surface of the Earth that lies opposite the Prime Meridian and offsets the date as one travels east or west across it), Chatham Island (lying off the east coast of the South Island) and the town of Gisborne (on the eastern side of North Island) are among the first settlements in the world to see the dawn of a new day.

Left: **A rocky beach along the Hauraki Gulf of the North Island.**

Opposite: **Aerial view of Waterfall Bay (*left*), Mistletoe Bay (*right*) and Kenepuru Sound (*top*).**

A snow-capped view of Mount Taranaki from across the plains during autumn.

Aoraki/Mount Cook, in the Southern Alps, is the tallest mountain in New Zealand. Standing at a majestic 12,316 feet (3,754 m), it has inspired Maori people to call it Aorangi (ah-or-rung-ee), the "cloud piercer." There are more than 200 named peaks that are higher than 7,500 feet (2,286 m) in New Zealand.

MOUNTAINS, GLACIERS, AND FJORDS

On the geological time scale, New Zealand is a relatively young country, with most of the modern landscape having developed within the last 10 million years. Huge land upheavals that occurred deep in the Earth 20 million years ago and even earlier caused the mountains to be pushed up gradually. At least 75 percent of the land is 650 feet (200 m) above sea level. The height of the Southern Alps, a massive mountain range that runs almost the entire length of the South Island's western side, continues to grow even today at the same rate as human fingernails.

Mount Taranaki (also known as Mount Egmont) is a dormant stratovolcano (a volcano composed of both lava flows and pyroclastic material) with a symmetrical cone that stands in splendid isolation on the west coast of the lower North Island. According to Maori mythology, Mount Taranaki once resided in the center of the North Island, along with all the other New Zealand volcanoes. He wooed and won the wife of Tongariro, another mountain. After a great battle involving fire, steam, and rock-hurling, Taranaki was banished to the west coast. The path of his escape is said to be marked by the Wanganui River.

The mountains were eroded by glaciers (slow-moving masses of ice) during the Ice Age (a period of long-term reduction in the temperature of Earth's climate that led to an expansion of the continental ice sheets, polar ice sheets, and alpine glaciers), which began about 2.5 million years ago. These glaciers (there are 360 of them in the Southern Alps) carved out the fjords (long, narrow inlets of the sea that lie between steep cliffs) and valleys (long depressions in the surface of the land that usually contain a river) around most of the South Island lakes and rivers, and deposited sediment to form rich alluvial plains, which run down to the sea. The largest, Tasman Glacier, is 18 miles (29 km) long. The fjords are found in the southwestern region of the South Island in an area covered by Fjordland National Park, one of the largest national parks in the world.

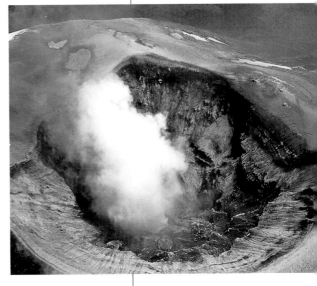

VOLCANOES AND EARTHQUAKES

New Zealand is positioned on the southwest corner of the so-called "Ring of Fire." This is the area around the rim of the Pacific Ocean where huge sections of the Earth's crust called plates collide, causing intense volcanic and earthquake activity.

Compared with other countries on the Pacific Rim, such as Japan, the Philippines, and Chile, New Zealand experiences only moderate volcanic and earthquake activity, although minor earthquakes are common. The most disastrous earthquake in recent times occurred in the North Island town of Napier in 1931, when the entire town and the surrounding villages were destroyed and 258 people were killed.

There are many volcanoes in New Zealand, but most of them are extinct. A volcanic plateau covers most of the central North Island, where the mountains of the Tongariro National Park rise. These mountains include three active volcanoes—Ruapehu, Ngauruhoe, and Tongariro.

Mount Ruapehu, the tallest mountain on the North Island in the Tongariro National Park, is a volcano that erupted during 2006 and 2007. These volcanic eruptions were accompanied by earthquakes measuring 2.9 on the Richter scale. The 2007 eruption seriously disrupted the ski season and killed one person.

Lake Taupo is tranquil today, but nearly 2,000 years ago, its violent birth spewed 15,000 times the volume of material ejected when Mount Saint Helens in Washington State erupted in 1980.

LAKES AND RIVERS

There are at least 20 large lakes in New Zealand and many smaller ones. Lake Taupo in the central North Island is by far the largest, with a surface area of 234 square miles (606 square km). It was formed by an enormous volcanic eruption in A.D. 181 during which an incredible 3,600 cubic miles (15,000 cubic km) of ash and pumice fell virtually all over the North Island.

The magnificent alpine settings and large lakes in the southwestern region of the South Island attract many visitors. Some artificial lakes have been created on both the North and South islands to service hydroelectric projects. Numerous rivers speed their way down from the mountains to the sea. Because they flow so fast, they have become an important source of hydroelectric power. The longest river is the Waikato on the North Island, which flows 264 miles (425 km) into the Tasman Sea.

LOWLANDS

The most extensive flat area in New Zealand, the Canterbury Plains, lies along the eastern coast of the South Island. This is one of the richest farming areas because the soil is the result of millions of years of glacial deposits. Farms here are the country's main suppliers of wheat and grain, while the many sheep farms have made the area famous for "Canterbury Lamb" (New Zealand lamb that is exported—either chilled or frozen). There are also coastal plains in the Southland and Otago provinces.

A number of coastal plains are found in the North Island: Bay of Plenty province (New Zealand) produces dairy cattle, seafood, and a wide range of subtropical crops, while East Cape produces the bulk of the country's corn. East Cape, Hawke's Bay, and Marlborough in the South Island all have vineyards and orchards.

THERMAL REGION

From the south of Lake Taupo to White Island (an active volcano in the Bay of Plenty) is a belt of geysers (springs that discharge hot water and steam), boiling mud pools, and hot-water springs. One of these, Frying Pan Lake, is the world's largest geyser. The spring has a surface area of 45,450 square yards (38,000 square m), and at the spring's deepest point the temperature reaches 389°F (200°C). Much of the thermal activity takes place in and around the city of Rotorua on the central North Island, located on the banks of southern shore of Lake Rotorua.

These thermal pools, found in Rotorua, are popular with visitors from all over the world.

Only two other countries have geysers—Iceland and the United States. Geysers occur in areas where water from lakes and rivers seeps down into concentrations of hot rock, heats up rapidly in a confined space, and then explodes up through vents, emitting boiling water and steam. The water expelled by the geysers contains dissolved minerals that solidify into colorful and shapely silica formations on nearby surfaces as the water evaporates. It is claimed that the minerals in thermal waters are beneficial to the health. Rotorua has been a therapeutic bathing center of international repute since the late 19th century.

Cracked mud during a drought at the Miranda Nature Reserve in Waikato.

CLIMATE

New Zealand's ocean environment keeps the climate mild, but the mountains, together with the prevailing westerly winds, cause marked differences in temperature and rainfall from west to east. This is particularly so in the South Island, where westerly winds cause the clouds to draw moisture from the sea. As they rise, the clouds hit the mountains and rain is released onto the west coast. Fjordland is one of the wettest areas in the world. Drought often occurs on the east coast of both islands in summer (December–February). However, there is usually plenty of rain throughout the country, with winter (June–August) being the wettest season in the North Island and spring (September–November) being the wettest season on the South Island's west coast. The provinces of Auckland and Northland enjoy a year-round subtropical climate where citrus fruit is grown.

Mean annual temperatures range from 61°F (16°C) in Northland to 50°F (10°C) in the southernmost part of the country. The highest temperatures occur east of the mountain ranges in summer, creating hot and dry conditions, while the lowest temperatures occur during winter in the mountains and in the inland areas of Canterbury and Otago. There are few places where temperatures higher than 86°F (30°C) or lower than 14°F (–10°C) occur. Snow falls mainly in the mountains, but during the coldest month of the year (July), snow often falls for a few days in the eastern coastal provinces of the South Island.

FLORA AND FAUNA

Before New Zealand was inhabited by people, the land was covered in forest and "bush" (evergreen broadleaf trees and enormous tree ferns, ground ferns, and clinging vines). In the forests, native trees such as *rimu* (ri-moo), *totara* (TOR-tah-rah), and *kauri* (kah-oo-ree) grew to spectacular heights.

When the Maori people came to New Zealand from eastern Polynesia around 1,100 years ago, they cleared one-third of the forests, and later (in the early 19th century), the European settlers cleared another third. Today only 23 percent of New Zealand's original forest cover remains. Other tree species have been introduced, and the plantation forests now include radiata pine, elm, birch, poplar, macrocarpa, and beech.

Coastal wetlands have other forms of native vegetation, as well as marine birds such as oystercatchers and migratory waders. Mangrove trees grow in swamps, mudflats, estuaries, and tidal creeks in Northland. New Zealand shrubland contains the highest proportion of tree-sized daisies and plants with interlocking and twisted branches in the world. In the grasslands, toitoi, pampas, and flax plants can be found. These were cultivated by the early Maori and were used to make baskets and clothing, thatching for houses, and ropes, sails, and rigging for ships.

Because New Zealand was cut off from the rest of the world by its oceans over 80 million years ago, only mammals that could fly were able to reach it. The only native land mammal in New Zealand is the bat; other land mammals were introduced by the Maori and European settlers.

Mount Cook National Park. Areas of New Zealand that have beautiful, unique, or scientifically important natural features, or that contain rare or endangered animals and plants, are preserved and protected as national parks.

13

MOA

The various species of Moa were flightless birds that were native to New Zealand. The largest species, the giant moa, reached about 12 feet (4 m) in height and weighed about 550 pounds (249 kg). They were the dominant herbivores in the New Zealand forest ecosystem for thousands of years and were hunted only by the Haast's eagle. All species are generally believed to have become extinct by A.D. 1500, mainly due to hunting by Maori.

Nearly all of New Zealand's native species of reptiles and amphibians live only here and nowhere else in the world. New Zealand's native frogs lay eggs that turn directly into frogs without first becoming free-swimming tadpoles. They have tail-wagging muscles, but no tails. They do not croak like normal frogs do; instead they let out a thin, high-pitched squeak. They are among the world's most ancient frogs.

In the absence of other mammals and many predators, birdlife in New Zealand was, and still is, amazing. New Zealand is an avian wonderland, with many species evolving to take over niches that would normally be occupied by mammals.

Of the 44 reptile species that are native to New Zealand, the *tuatara* (too-uh-tah-ruh) is the largest, growing up to 2 feet (60 cm) long. It is the only surviving species of a family of reptiles that became extinct in other parts of the world 60 million years ago. Found

Before mammals were introduced, flightless birds (including very large species) were able to exist without threat. This bird is a kea (ke-uh), and it is the only alpine parrot found in the world.

only on New Zealand's offshore islands, the tuatara (which resembles an iguana) has traces of what was once a third eye. Tuataras are aggressive predators, ambushing their prey with spectacular bursts of speed and strength. They are one of the rarest reptiles on Earth.

An even more ancient "living fossil" is New Zealand's *weta* (we-tah), a wingless insect that has hardly changed at all over the last 190 million years. The harmless giant weta is the heaviest insect in the world, weighing up to 2.5 ounces (71 g), almost as much as a thrush.

New Zealand also has one of the world's largest gecko lizards, Duvaucel's gecko (*H. duvaucelii*). New Zealand geckos are unusual because they give birth to live young—usually twins—rather than laying eggs. The only other geckos that do this live in New Caledonia (an island situated 1,056 miles [1,700 km] from New Zealand).

THE KIWI

The *kiwi* (kee-wee), a large, nocturnal, shy, flightless bird, has a long slender bill with nostrils at the tip. It lays only one egg at a time. In relation to the bird's body size, the kiwi's egg is the largest in the world, weighing approximately one-third of the female bird's weight. After the egg is laid, the male partner incubates and rears the young. The kiwi is the only bird that has a sense of smell. Its name comes from the male bird's distinctive, shrill call. The kiwi is a well-known emblem of New Zealand, and it appears on the country's one-dollar coin. *Kiwi* is also a popular nickname for a New Zealander.

A scene from the South Island province of Canterbury. New Zealand's population of 4.25 million (about the same as Los Angeles) is very small compared to other countries of similar land size. Japan, for example, has a population of 127.8 million. Some 85 percent of New Zealanders live in centers with 1,000 or more people. Only 15 percent live in rural areas.

PROVINCES AND CITIES

When the European settlers came to New Zealand in the early 19th century, they settled mainly in the South Island. But for the last 100 years, people have been drifting north, and now 3.4 million people (80 percent of the population) live in the North Island, with 51 percent concentrated in the provinces of Northland, Auckland, Waikato, and Bay of Plenty, where the climate is warmer.

There are four main urban centers in New Zealand: Auckland and Wellington in the North Island and Christchurch and Dunedin in the South Island.

AUCKLAND, New Zealand's largest urban area, occupies the isthmus between the Hauraki Gulf on the east coast and the Manukau Harbor on the west coast. With about one boat for every four households, Auckland has earned the name "City of Sails." A city of 1.3 million inhabitants, it is the most cosmopolitan place in the country and is the main tourist and trade gateway.

WELLINGTON, the capital of New Zealand, is located near the southern end of the North Island. It is the second-largest urban area, with a population of 448,956. Wellington Harbor in Port Nicholson covers 7 square miles (18 square km) and is considered one of the finest natural harbors in the world.

CHRISTCHURCH is situated on the Canterbury Plains. It has a population of 359,900. Early English settlers were successful in re-creating an English society here. This is reflected in the city's English layout, which has a stone, Gothic-style Anglican cathedral that dominates a central square. (Gothic architecture flourished in Europe during the 11th–14th century—the high- and late-medieval period.)

DUNEDIN has a population of 119,000 and is located at the top of the long, fjordlike Otago Harbor. Settled originally by people from Scotland, Dunedin was named after the old Celtic name of Edinburgh, Dun Edin. It is sometimes called the Edinburgh of the South. It is here that New Zealand's only whiskey is distilled.

HISTORY

AS THE LAST SIGNIFICANT LANDMASS in the world to be populated, New Zealand has a relatively short history. Until the late 19th century the inhabitants of New Zealand, known as the Maori, had transferred their history down through the generations largely by word of mouth. Some events may have become distorted over time, but there are some things that are known for certain.

Europeans first sighted New Zealand in the 17th century, and by the early 19th century, British settlers had arrived. New Zealand became a British colony in 1840 with the signing of the Waitangi Treaty. By 1907 it was a dominion in the British Empire. Although New Zealand has now become less dependent on Britain, it remains a member of the British Commonwealth.

The British Commonwealth, also called the Commonwealth of Nations, is a voluntary association of 53 independent sovereign states, most of which are former British colonies (the exceptions are the United Kingdom itself and Mozambique).

Left: **A replica of an early Maori canoe. Maoridom was previously divided into 42 distinct tribal groups, each known by their individual tribal names. Later, to distinguish themselves from the Europeans, they called themselves Maori, meaning "ordinary" or "usual."**

Opposite: **A lion statue stands in front of the war memorial cenotaph in the capital city of Wellington.**

A picture depicting early Maori life. Tribal warfare was not uncommon, and after the fierce conflict, the Maori would eat their defeated enemies. Young women and children were often taken as slaves.

EARLY ARRIVALS

The first people to come to New Zealand, in about the 10th century A.D., were from eastern Polynesia (a large grouping of more than 1,000 islands scattered over the central and southern Pacific Ocean known to natives as Hawaiki). Some historians believe there was a "Great Migration" at one point in time, while other evidence suggests that numerous canoe voyages from Hawaiki brought groups of Polynesians to New Zealand over a period of hundreds of years. The occupants of these famous canoes became the founders of the Maori tribes that still exist today.

According to a Maori legend, the very first voyager to reach New Zealand, in about A.D. 950, was a man called Kupe. He named the country *Aotearoa* (ah-or-te-ah-roar), which means "land of the long white cloud." Before Kupe arrived, there was no human habitation on the islands.

PRE-EUROPEAN MAORI

The Maori brought with them dogs, rats, and edible plants. They subsisted by fishing, hunting (especially the giant moa bird and seals), and gathering plants. Maori people were also horticulturalists, growing their own crops, such as *kumara* (KOO-mah-rah), a sweet potato. When the Maori came to temperate and cold New Zealand, they found it very difficult to raise some of the plants on which tropical Polynesians depended. They came to depend heavily on other food sources, such as fern roots. They grouped themselves into extended families, subtribes with up to 500 members, and larger tribes. Each tribe lived in a village, usually within the reach of an earthwork fort, or *pa* (PAA).

Tribal land, valued for the food it could produce, such as mutton birds, or its natural resources, such as greenstone, was presided over by tribal chiefs and jealously guarded. Although tribes did trade their various regional commodities, intertribal warfare was a way of gaining control over the best land. It also gave *mana* (mah-nah), or prestige and honor, to the chiefs.

EUROPEAN DISCOVERY

The Dutch navigator Abel Tasman was the first European to sight New Zealand, in December 1642. He called it "Staten Landt," but it was soon renamed "Nieuw Zealand" after a Dutch province. Unfortunately, when Tasman attempted to land, the local Maori thought his trumpet fanfare was a call to war and Tasman lost four men. He sailed away without ever landing and never came back.

Europeans did not return to New Zealand until 1769, when Captain James Cook, an English explorer, was sent to the South Pacific on a scientific expedition. He circumnavigated the country and thoroughly surveyed its coastline. His good reports encouraged whalers and traders to come to New Zealand. Other explorers began to arrive, including the French, Italians, and Americans.

By the late 18th century there were probably about 150,000 Maori living in Aotearoa, nearly all of them in the warmer North Island. Although they were naturally suspicious of the early Europeans, the Maori were quick to see the advantages in trading with the Europeans, particularly to gain muskets for tribal warfare.

A hand engraving of Captain James Cook. He was later killed by the natives in Hawaii in 1779 on his third expedition to the Pacific Ocean.

NEW ARRIVALS

Three Christian missionary families formed the first organized European settlement in the country. The Reverend Samuel Marsden arrived from England in 1814 and preached his first sermon in the Bay of Islands on Christmas Day that year. By 1838 the Bishop Jean-Baptiste Pompallier had founded a Roman Catholic mission in the same area.

The vision of the early missionaries was one of a Christian and Maori New Zealand. However, commercial interests dominated subsequent developments.

The original Bay of Islands church. Missionaries introduced European technology and agricultural skills and, thus, expected to gain favor and prestige with the Maori people. They also hoped to influence trade between the whalers and the Maori. But the sophisticated Maori chiefs got the best deals and directly controlled trade.

In 1839 Edward Gibbon Wakefield formed the New Zealand Company. It was directed by influential men in London commerce, who were eager to get the New Zealand economy going. They dispatched settlers to Aotearoa and profited by selling their newly acquired land to them.

By the 1840s there were about 2,000 Europeans living in small settlements in New Zealand. Scattered throughout the country was a large transient population of whalers and traders. The Maori population, divided into independent tribes, had hardly changed since the late 1700s. The Maori traded extensively and successfully with the Europeans.

There was, however, no national government and no single set of formal laws. Maori land was being sold in a disorganized way. Some British settlers feared that New Zealand might be taken over by France, so both Maori and Pakeha groups asked Britain to provide some sort of protection and law and order.

INDEPENDENCE AND A TREATY

Great Britain accepted the Maori chiefs' request to recognize their independence, while at the same time extending British protection to New Zealand. It was hoped that British resident James Busby would bring about law and order in the country. Unfortunately he lacked the means to enforce his authority and, as more and more immigrants arrived in New Zealand, disagreements between Maori and Pakeha began to threaten lives and trade. Busby was replaced by William Hobson, a naval captain, who was sent to New Zealand in January 1840 to negotiate with the Maori for the sovereignty of the country.

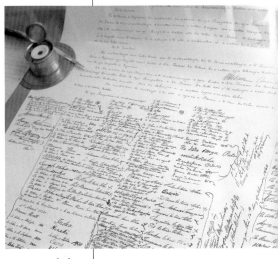

Britain decided to make New Zealand a colony in order to control the European settlers and protect the rights of the Maori people. Hobson, Busby, and the missionary Henry Williams conceived the idea of drawing up a treaty that would be acceptable to both the British Crown and the Maori chiefs. On February 6, 1840, at Waitangi in the Bay of Islands, a treaty was read in English and Maori to more than 400 Maori. After much debate and on the advice of Williams, the Maori chiefs agreed to give Queen Victoria of England sovereignty over their land. They accepted her protection and the offer of the same rights and duties of citizenship as the people of England, while still retaining their lands, forests, fisheries, and other possessions. More than 40 signatures or marks were appended

For the Maori people, the Treaty of Waitangi recognized that in exchange for settlement rights, their natural rights as original occupants would be upheld. For the European settlers, the treaty allowed them to emigrate peacefully to New Zealand under the British flag.

to the Maori text of the treaty, mostly by chiefs around the Bay of Islands. The Maori version of the Treaty of Waitangi was eventually signed by more than 500 chiefs.

LAND WARS

At first the treaty was recognized and observed as a contract that was binding on both parties, and in 1852 Britain allowed New Zealand to be self-governing. As people continued to migrate to New Zealand, there was increasing demand for land, and the Maori people became cautious about selling their land cheaply to investors who profited from the arrival of settlers.

The law seemed to favor the Pakeha. Conflict between settlers and the Maori finally led to land wars in the 1860s and the emergence of united tribes in the central North Island that had their own king. (The area is still known today as King Country.) Thousands of British troops were dispatched to control the Maori. During the land wars, the Maori won much admiration for their superb fighting and skill. During the Battle of Gate Pa (a *pa* is a fortified settlement), a Maori force of about 235 warriors defeated a combined British regiment and naval brigade of approximately 2,000 men who were much better armed than the Maori. However, the Maori eventually lost the war and their land due to the superior firepower of the British troops and the ever-continuing arrival of European settlers. It was at this point that New Zealand became a British colony in reality, not just on paper.

GROWING PROSPERITY

Peace was not restored until 1870. Meanwhile the discovery of gold in 1861 at Gabriel's Gully, Otago, a province in the South Island, marked the

A tombstone commemorating soldiers who died in the Maori land wars of the 1860s.

New Zealand and Australian troops bound for Europe during World War I.

beginning of a major gold rush in New Zealand. A flood of new settlers came to the South Island, which was relatively untroubled by land disputes. The gold rush was over by the 1870s, but by then, agricultural industries had developed that could employ the growing population. Railways and roads were built so that produce could be transported to the coast and shipped all over the world. The invention of refrigeration in the 1880s meant that meat and dairy products could travel as far as England.

DEVELOPING A SENSE OF NATIONHOOD

New Zealand became a dominion in 1907. At the outbreak of World War I in 1914, the country remained loyal to Britain by sending troops to Europe. New Zealand lost 17,000 men from a population of only one million, largely due to a badly organized campaign by the British in Turkey. New Zealanders became disenchanted with the "motherland," and a sense of separate nationhood began to grow.

There were several outstanding men of Maori and mixed Maori-Pakeha ancestry who were leading members of Parliament and prominent intellectuals. Sir Apirana Turupa Ngata was a prominent New Zealand politician and lawyer who was also known for his work in protecting

Michael Joseph Savage was the leader of the Parliament and prime minister of New Zealand's first government.

Maori language and culture. His portrait is on the New Zealand 50-dollar note. Te Rangi Hiroa (Peter Buck) was a doctor who worked successfully with another Maori lawyer, Sir Maui Wiremu Pita Naera Pomare, to improve Maori health and living conditions. Both men were members of Parliament.

By the interwar period, many New Zealanders were proud of what they saw as their country's unique achievements in race relations. This, in turn, was one of the foundations for a belief that New Zealand had a special national role in the Pacific, and in the administration of other Polynesian peoples.

New Zealand administered the Cook Islands, Niue, Tokelau, and Western Samoa (taking the last from the Germans during World War I). Although Western Samoa became the first Pacific island country to gain independence, the Cook Islands and Niue remain states in "free association" with New Zealand, and the Tokelauans voted to remain a New Zealand colony in 2007.

A period of industrial progress followed during the 1920s, but the worldwide Great Depression (a dramatic, worldwide economic downturn that began in some countries as early as 1929 and lasted until about 1939) hit New Zealand severely. The Labour Party, which had been formed out of various labor and trade unions and radical movements, won an election and formed its first government in 1935 under Michael Joseph Savage, leader of the Parliamentary Labour Party and prime minister of New Zealand.

A number of social reforms followed, including a social security system, a national health service, and a low-rent state housing program. The National Party also emerged during this period to represent more conservative and rural interests. It won the general election in 1949.

Since 1949 the Labour and National parties have competed in elections to form the government. The Labour Party has held power for 22 years and the National Party for 35 years, sometimes in coalition with minor parties.

The early post–World War II years saw a boom in New Zealand because of higher prices for wool as well as other agricultural products. The Korean War was on, and there was a demand for blankets in that country. The boom ended with the end of the Korean War in 1953.

Changes in the world economy during the 1960s and 1970s threatened New Zealand's high standard of living. When Britain joined the European Economic Community (an organization established by a treaty signed in 1957 by Belgium, France, Italy, Luxembourg, the Netherlands, and West Germany [now Germany]) in 1973, New Zealand lost its guaranteed access on favorable terms to England, its largest overseas market. That same year a worldwide oil crisis threatened oil supplies to New Zealand and, from 1974 on, the impact of much higher world oil prices was felt. New Zealand's traditional economic and political relations were challenged.

In 1975 a leader emerged who was determined to tackle the economic crisis. Robert Muldoon, the new National Party prime minister, extended government protection to the manufacturing industry and increased government funding to the troubled farming sector. To help the economy grow, his government funded an array of expensive "Think Big" projects. To counter inflation, Muldoon assumed increasing

Robert Muldoon during the 1975 elections rally. With his abrasive style and quick wit, he dominated both the Parliament and his own cabinet ministers, concentrating economic and political power in his own hands.

27

THE RAINBOW WARRIOR

In 1985 the Greenpeace (a global environmental organization) flagship *Rainbow Warrior* lay anchored in Auckland Harbor, preparing to sail to Moruroa near Tahiti to protest French nuclear testing. The ill-fated ship never left Auckland, as saboteurs hired by the French government secretly attached explosives to the side of the ship and sank it, killing Dutch freelance photographer Fernando Pereira. The attack was a public relations disaster for France, after it was quickly exposed by the New Zealand police. In 1987 the French government agreed to pay New Zealand $13 million (in New Zealand dollars) as compensation and formally apologized for the bombing. The French government also paid 2.3 million in French francs as compensation to the family of the killed photographer.

A dominion is a self-governing country that is a member of the British Empire. A colony, on the other hand, is ruled directly by the British government.

control over all aspects of the economy. By 1984 the government was settling all prices and wages, as well as interest rates and the exchange rate between the New Zealand dollar and other currencies. New Zealand had become one of the most centrally controlled economies in the world.

CRISIS

Huge and growing economic and political pressures resulted. In 1984 Muldoon called for a general election, in which his National Party lost to the Labour Party. The new government faced a massive economic crisis.

The New Zealand dollar was devalued and, over the next six years, the Labour government began a major program of deregulation and financial reform. By the early 1990s the World Bank and other international organizations said that New Zealand had one of the most deregulated and least centrally controlled economies in the world.

NUCLEAR-FREE NEW ZEALAND

By reducing the role of government, the Labour government of 1984 to 1990 departed from many traditional Labour Party policies. On one subject, however, it held true to its election promises: a nuclear-free New Zealand. The government refused to accept visits from American or other warships that might be carrying nuclear weapons or that were nuclear-powered.

HELEN ELIZABETH CLARK

When the New Zealand Labour Party came into office as part of a coalition following the 1999 election, Helen Elizabeth Clark became the second female prime minister of New Zealand. During her term in office, women have held a number of prominent positions in New Zealand, such as the queen of England, governor-general, speaker of the House of Representatives, and chief justice.

Clark's government has brought significant changes to the New Zealand welfare system, such as child tax credits. Her government has also changed industrial relations law and raised the minimum wage six times. Interests on student loans have been abolished as well. One controversial bill passed during Clark's term in office is the anti-smacking bill, which makes it illegal for parents to hit their children.

Labour Prime Minister David Russell Lange made the nuclear-free position his personal crusade. Eventually increasing tensions within the Labour government over the reforms and their impact on the poor marred the later years of Lange's leadership. Lange resigned as prime minister in 1990 and the Labour Party lost the 1990 and 1993 elections to the National Party.

A reformed National Party, free of the influence of Robert Muldoon, continued the reform process and built on the growing acceptance at home and abroad of both New Zealand's radical economic reforms and its nuclear-free position. The National Party lost the 1999 election to the Labour Party, under the leadership of Helen Elizabeth Clark .

NEW ZEALAND IN THE WORLD TODAY

New Zealand is committed to international security, and its focus is more on peace support operations than participation in war. New Zealand currently has more than 400 Defense Force personnel and 75 police deployed in peace support missions in 14 countries. Addressing instability in the Pacific is a high priority for New Zealand, because New Zealand is a Pacific nation and because it shares close cultural, family, and political links with all the islands of the region. New Zealand's defense forces have been engaged in efforts to stabilize and rebuild states after periods of conflict or fragility, and over the past few years, it has been engaged in the Solomon Islands, Timor-Leste, Bougainville, and Tonga.

GOVERNMENT

NEW ZEALAND IS AN INDEPENDENT state with a democratic form of government. It is a member of the British Commonwealth, the Asia-Pacific Economic Cooperation (APEC), and the United Nations (UN) and associated bodies.

HEAD OF STATE

The formal head of the state of New Zealand is Queen Elizabeth II of Britain. The queen is represented in New Zealand by the governor-general, who is appointed by the queen on the advice of the New Zealand government, normally for three to five years. Early governor-generals were often nobles from England. More recently they have been distinguished New Zealanders.

Above: **Britain's Queen Elizabeth II arrives in Wellington, New Zealand on her Golden Jubilee tour.**

Opposite: **The Richard John Seddon statue stands in front of the Parliament building in Wellington.**

As the queen's representative, the governors-general opens Parliament, formally appoints the prime minister and other ministers, and signs legislation passed by Parliament. The governor-general has no discretion in such matters. He or she accepts the advice of the prime minister and the government that is in power. Only where there is no clear control of Parliament, and, thus, no clear government, would the governor-general have more than a nominal role to play.

In recent years there has been some discussion about whether New Zealand should become a republic, replacing the sovereign with a government-appointed head of state. This would effectively raise the governor-general to the status of president, rather than a representative of the queen. Opinion polls indicate that most New Zealanders prefer to retain the queen as head of state.

AN UNUSUALLY SIMPLE STRUCTURE

New Zealand has perhaps one of the simplest structures of government of any advanced nation.

NO WRITTEN CONSTITUTION Like Britain, New Zealand is a parliamentary sovereignty. In other words, the will of Parliament rules supreme. The laws that Parliament makes are the rule of law for the country, and the role of the courts is only to interpret them.

NO SEPARATION OF POWERS The party or coalition of parties that controls Parliament decides who will be appointed as prime minister and other ministers. Each minister is given an area or areas of responsibility. The departments, which are part of the executive branch of government, that cover each area report to and are responsible to the minister in charge of that area. In other words, the group that controls Parliament also controls the executive. The judiciary is independent, but it cannot overturn laws passed by Parliament. Thus it is also subject to the laws passed by the group that controls Parliament.

ONLY ONE CHAMBER OF PARLIAMENT   In 1950 the second chamber of Parliament was abolished. The single chamber that was retained consists of elected members of Parliament. Control of this body, which is won in elections, gives the winners control of Parliament.

LOCAL GOVERNMENT RELATIVELY UNIMPORTANT Local and regional government accounts for less than 2 percent of the gross domestic product (GDP) of New Zealand. Unlike in many countries, local authorities have no direct role in the provision of education or health services—these are the responsibility of the central government.

Elected local and regional government bodies are responsible for sewage, water supply, flood control, local roads (but not national highways), planning controls (for example, changes in land use and building permits), and provision of optional local leisure facilities, such as a sports stadium.

Until recently local authorities have controlled ports and electricity distribution. This is no longer required by law, and many local authorities have sold or partly sold their interest to private owners. The main source of revenue for local and regional governments is property tax.

FIRST-PAST-THE-POST ELECTORAL SYSTEM
Until the October 1996 general election, members were elected to Parliament by direct election from constituencies around the country. This usually meant that one party would win control of Parliament.

In this winner-take-all system, known in New Zealand as a first-past-the-post electoral system, votes cast for losing candidates were not reflected

Taxes are always a contentious issue in elections.

in the makeup of Parliament. Unhappiness with this system eventually resulted in a call for change from a first-past-the-post electoral system to one of proportional representation (an electoral system that aims at a close match between the percentage of votes that a group of candidates obtains in an election and the percentage of seats the group receives).

A NEW ELECTORAL SYSTEM

In two referenda held in 1992 and 1993, New Zealanders voted to adopt a system of proportional representation for Parliament called "mixed-member proportional" (MMP).

Under the old system, minor parties could gain a significant minority of votes, but still could not win any individual seats in Parliament. Under MMP the number of seats that a party gains in Parliament is dictated by the proportion of the vote it receives nationally.

ELECTION RESULTS: FIRST MIXED-MEMBER PROPORTIONAL GOVERNMENT

Thanks to the efforts of Kate Sheppard, on September 19, 1893, New Zealand became the first country in the world to grant women the right to vote.

The first MMP election, held in October 1996, left a third party, New Zealand First, holding the balance of power between the Labour and National parties. After lengthy negotiations, New Zealand First entered a formal coalition with the National Party in December 1996. Jim Bolger, the leader of the National Party, remained prime minister.

PARLIAMENT

Parliament is responsible for making laws, voting "supply" (finance) to the government, and appointing the ministerial heads of the executive.

Proposed laws are placed before Parliament in the form of bills. These are debated both on the floor of the house and generally by a subcommittee of Members of Parliament (MPs). A successful bill has to pass through three "readings," or votes, in Parliament, before being sent to the governor-general for signature and passage into law. Most bills are introduced by the government of the day, although the opposition or individual MPs may also seek to introduce bills.

Each year the budget contains the government's proposals for expenditure and revenue-raising. This is specified in great detail in budget documents prepared by the treasury for the government. Until recently the budget has been voted on in its entirety by the government-controlled majority of MPs. Individual MPs were not permitted to make proposals for changes to the budget.

However, as part of the move toward proportional representation, these rules have been changed so that individual MPs can make such proposals, as long as they do not significantly alter the budget. New Zealand is the first country with an advanced economy to allow its Parliament to do this.

A REFORMED EXECUTIVE

Executive governmental functions are carried out under the control of the ministers appointed by the governor-general. In practice these ministers are chosen by the party or parties that control Parliament.

There are some 38,000 staff employed by public service departments. The public service was substantially reorganized as part of widespread economic reforms in the 1980s. These reforms have greatly increased

Most matters are settled along party lines, with the party leadership deciding how members of that party should vote. On some issues, however, MPs vote according to their conscience—for instance, private members' bills to permit casinos have passed and bills to allow euthanasia have been rejected.

PRIVATIZATION

Many public-sector trading activities, including New Zealand Telecom and Post Bank, have been sold to the private sector. Of those that remain, many have been formed into State-Owned Enterprises (SOEs). These are commercial bodies run by directors with extensive business experience. The objective is to make a profit, with the government as a shareholder. The idea is to keep ministers' involvement with SOEs to a minimum. In practice key SOE decisions (for example, decisions over electricity charges) are politically sensitive and tend to trigger ministers' involvement.

Although reforms have increased accountability, they have also reduced loyalty and the amount of experience in the public sector, with junior staff and chief executives alike tending to move between departments and in and out of the public service.

flexibility and accountability and sharpened efficiency. Under the State Sector Act of 1988, the chief executive of each public department is now accountable for running his or her department efficiently and effectively, and agrees on a contract of performance with the minister in charge of that department.

In this contractual relationship between ministers and department chief executives, the ministers decide what results they want and how much money is available. As in private sector firms, chief executives determine how they will accomplish the job. They have a large degree of freedom in this role.

Financial reforms in the Public Finance Act and elsewhere have required public departments to provide a high standard of financial disclosure, for instance, in distinguishing current expenditure from capital (investment) expenditure.

In public sector reforms and accountability, New Zealand is recognized as a world leader. Its system has been studied extensively by overseas delegations and international bodies.

THE JUDICIARY

Judges interpret and apply the law, and the judiciary is independent of the government. Aside from a system of district courts and the High Court, there are various specialist tribunals and courts in New Zealand. Most notable are the Employment Court (which considers employment disputes) and the Waitangi Tribunal (which considers claims arising under the Treaty of Waitangi).

The most senior court in New Zealand is the Court of Appeal. Appeals from lower courts can be made to this body, while appeals from the Court of Appeal can be made to the Privy Council in England. However, the Privy Council, in reaching its verdicts, is bound by New Zealand statute. In 2004 the Supreme Court replaced the Judicial Committee of the Privy Council in London as New Zealand's highest court of appeal.

PRIVY COUNCIL The word *privy* means "private" or "secret." Thus a privy council was originally a committee of the monarch's closest advisors, who provided confidential advice on affairs of state. The privy council today hears appeals and judgments that were made before January 1, 2004.

The main form of law in New Zealand is New Zealand statute law—the law passed by the New Zealand Parliament. Subject to this are three other forms of law: common law (case law based on general rules developed by the courts, not only in New Zealand, but also, where relevant, in England and in other Commonwealth countries), United Kingdom statutes, and subordinate legislation (New Zealand statute may delegate some law-making powers to the governor-general and to local government).

ECONOMY

NEW ZEALAND HAS AN ADVANCED ECONOMY. From the 1860s on, it has offered a high standard of living to most European settlers, so that an ordinary working-class family could enjoy meat on the table every day and a horse for transportation when these would have been nothing more than dreams for people in Europe. New Zealand's position, relative to other advanced economies, slowly declined during the 20th century. However, from the mid-1990s on, the New Zealand economy began to expand, and its GDP has grown a little faster than the OECD (Organization for Economic Cooperation and Development) average. Nonetheless the World Bank calculates that, allowing for differences in prices of consumable goods between New Zealand and other countries, the income per person in New Zealand in 2006 was equivalent to $25,874, slightly lower than the average income of Britain and two-thirds that of the United States.

The primary economic sector—agriculture, forestry, and fishing—accounts for around 10 percent of New Zealand's production and

Electricity prices in New Zealand are among the lowest in the world. This is because two-thirds of the supply comes from hydroelectric power. Cheap power is particularly important to the aluminum-smelting industry, since its major cost is electricity.

Left: **A flock of sheep grazing near the train station in Southlands, New Zealand.**

Opposite: **Conroy apricot trees at the Jackson Orchard in Otago.**

An aerial view of the Fergusson Container Wharf in the Auckland Harbor.

employment, and manufacturing accounts for about 20 percent. The lion's share of production and employment is in the service sector, especially tourism, which contributes 9.5 percent to the GDP. The tourism industry is New Zealand's largest foreign exchange earner.

THE REFORMS

The success of New Zealand's major economic reforms from the mid-1980s to the early 1990s is often debated, both domestically and internationally. New Zealand is viewed as a test case for radical reform. The reforms caused big structural changes in New Zealand, particularly since they followed a period of tight state control.

The reforms began with the removal of exchange and loan controls, the deregulation of financial markets, and fluctuation in the value of the New Zealand dollar. Subsidies to farmers were virtually eliminated, making New Zealand agriculture the least subsidized in the world. Import controls were removed and tariffs gradually reduced. Free trade with Australia was established in 1989. The domestic air market was opened up, and ports, coastal shipping, and road transportation were deregulated.

The public sector was reformed and the government's accounts were greatly improved, so that they resembled those of a large company. Government-owned trading activities were set up on commercial lines and, in many cases, sold. The government received some $9 billion from privatization between 1988 and 1995.

The Reserve Bank Act of 1989 made the central bank independent of the government, with the sole aim of monetary policy being price stability.

The last of the major reforms, the Employment Contracts Act of 1991, decentralized wage negotiations from industry and occupational level to the firm, which means that workers in an industry would negotiate directly with the firm they were working for concerning their wages. Trade union membership was made voluntary and workers could now choose which union would represent them, if any.

The aim of all these reforms was to improve the country's economic performance and the government's financial position. The main initial impact of the reforms was to increase efficiency, but, at the same time, to increase unemployment.

Forestry, mining, railways, postal services, telecommunications, electricity generation and transmission, and other areas were run as government departments with little concern for profit, return on investment, or for the customer.

A parking meter attendant on duty in New Zealand.

Under commercial pressures it was proved possible to run these services with far less staff. Typically employment fell by one-third to two-thirds. Organizations such as the postal services and railways moved from being loss-makers requiring frequent government subsidies to being profitable firms.

But tens of thousands of workers lost their jobs. Unemployment climbed from 4 percent in 1986 to a peak of 11 percent in 1991. Some rural communities and small towns were devastated, and the large supply of low-skilled but well-paying jobs that had characterized the

ROGER DOUGLAS—HERO OR TRAITOR?

As the Labour government's finance minister from 1984 to 1988, Roger Douglas was the primary architect of New Zealand's economic reforms, which became known as Rogernomics.

Because the reforms overturned traditional views about the role of government and led to job losses, he was regarded as a traitor by some Labour Party supporters. Nonetheless his reforms were welcomed by others, who believed they gave the country new hope for the future.

Douglas's proposals became increasingly radical and led to a split with Prime Minister Lange, who fired him. Douglas later left the Labour Party and helped form a new right-wing and reform-minded party called the Association of Consumers and Taxpayers (ACT), along with Derek Francis Quigley.

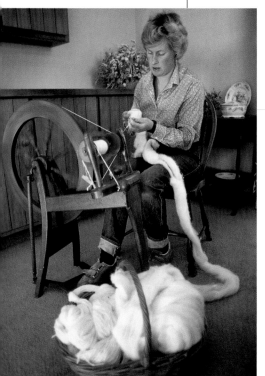

A woman spins wool at a farm. New Zealand is the world's largest producer of "strong wool," which is used mainly for carpets and blankets.

New Zealand economy for many decades was permanently depleted. Many traditional occupations and career paths vanished.

The removal of financial regulations led to a credit and banking boom in the cities. Speculative companies were launched and the stock market rocketed upward. However, the New York stock market crash of October 1987 brought New Zealand's financial bubble to an abrupt end. Many of the banks and financial companies lacked the expertise to make sound investments in the new environment. One big retail bank needed two large capital injections from the government to stay afloat.

Despite these problems, the deregulated economy offered new opportunities. The economy finally moved out of recession in 1993. Most of New Zealand's economic indicators are now good. Its recent past and expected future growth levels are better than those of most other advanced economies. Inflation and government debt are low, and the government has run a budget surplus for several years. Unemployment is below 5 percent. Private investment has replaced falling government investment.

In these terms, the economic reforms have been a success. However, concerns remain about investment and trade and the social impact of the reforms.

The term *Asia-Pacific Economic Cooperation* (*APEC*) refers to an intergovernmental forum that facilitates economic growth and prosperity, cooperation, trade, and investment in the Asia-Pacific region, and operates on the basis of nonbinding commitments, open dialogue, and equal respect for the views of all participants, regardless of the size of their economy.

MACROECONOMIC POLICY

After World War II, New Zealand fell into a pattern of high inflation—making New Zealand prices higher relative to those of its trading partners—and repeated currency devaluations, which restored New Zealand prices to a lower level, making exports more competitive.

As New Zealand's living standards started to fall behind those of other advanced countries, successive governments tried to meet voters' concerns and assist industry by spending more. As expenditure was consistently higher than its revenue, the government had to borrow more and more, and then had to pay interest on its debt. This pushed up government expenditure further, making it even more difficult to balance the books.

The government's net public debt peaked at $33 billion in 1992, or 51 percent of the GDP. With subsequent economic growth and restraints and efficiencies in government expenditure, the situation has improved rapidly. By 1996 net public debt fell to some $20 billion, or 32 percent of GDP.

The central bank has operated a tough anti-inflation policy that has worked, but at the price of high interest rates and exchange rates. In terms of real interest rates (the actual interest rate less inflation), New Zealand has tended to have the highest rates of inflation of any advanced economy. This has deterred domestic investment—the cost of borrowing in New Zealand being so high—but attracted funds from overseas. High exchange rates have made exports more expensive overseas and imports into New Zealand cheaper.

Fishermen in Tauranga. A typical catch could include mackerel, tuna, dory, and blue grenadier, some of which gets processed and exported to other countries.

FOREIGN INVESTMENT

New Zealand has mainly been targeted for investment in financial services, telecommunications, forestry, and some areas of manufacturing.

Major investments both in forestry and in the processing of forest products is being undertaken by large firms in New Zealand.

Since privatization began in 1988, major flows of foreign direct investment (where a company buys a controlling interest in a firm, rather than buying stock or lending money on set terms) have come to New Zealand. As a percentage of GDP, New Zealand has consistently attracted the highest levels of such investment of any advanced economy, often some $2 billion per year (3–4 percent of GDP).

Investment brings the capital, managerial skills, and contacts of overseas firms to New Zealand and demonstrates confidence in the economy. Many overseas managers work in New Zealand. The New Zealand seller (often the government) gains the sale price. But the sale means a loss of control to foreign investors, who will also look for a return on their investment.

TRADE

As a small economy, less than 1 percent the size of the U.S. economy, New Zealand is highly dependent on trade. With a relatively small workforce of 2.73 million, it has to specialize in certain industries and import many items, as there is insufficient manpower to cover all sectors of the economy.

For much of its history, the New Zealand economy has been dominated by the primary sectors of agriculture, fishing, forestry, and mining. In 1913 New Zealand's three main exports were (in descending order of importance) wool, meat, and dairy products. In 1983 the same three industries dominated exports, though dairy products had overtaken wool and meat. However, from the 1970s on, exports have diversified and now include forestry products, fish, and fruit. The manufacturing sector also grew in importance as an exporter, and tourism became a significant earner of foreign currency.

In 2006 total merchandise exports (excluding trade in services, such as tourism) were worth $26.8 billion, one-third from manufactured exports and two-thirds from primary sector exports (including food). Key earners of foreign currency were tourism—$6.4 billion from overseas visitors (estimated), dairy—$4.8 billion, meat—$3.6 billion, forestry—$1.6 billion, fish—$0.9 billion, wool—$0.5 billion, fruit and nuts—$0.9 billion, and aluminum—$1.2 billion.

Until the mid-1970s the main export market for New Zealand was Britain. Since then New Zealand has diversified. Six markets are now of roughly equal importance: Australia, North America, Japan, China, the European Union, and east Asia.

An abandoned copper mine. The mining and quarrying sector employs about 5,000 workers, thus creating jobs for many of the locals.

The Wooing Tree Vineyard during autumn in Otago. In recent years New Zealand wines have moved from being low-priced products sold only on the domestic market to international prize winners.

Many of New Zealand's primary and manufacturing exporters have had difficulty in establishing distinctive products overseas. Often New Zealand exports commodities that have been bought solely on price, with the purchaser being indifferent to who supplies the goods. This means that New Zealand is a "price taker," vulnerable to changes in world commodity markets.

However, as the economic reforms have taken effect, some firms and industries have developed distinctively new, high-value-added products. For example, a New Zealand manufacturer of dishwashers and washing machines successfully exports to Europe. A manufacturer of aluminum frames has a zero-fault work practice where no faults are tolerated at all. This system is extensively studied by visiting Japanese delegations. Sophisticated navigational equipment is sold to overseas navies and major airports. Live fish are exported to Japan so that they can be consumed fresh. Flower exports to east Asia are developing rapidly. New Zealand yacht designers and builders are internationally acclaimed. More such success stories will be needed to ensure that New Zealand's trade continues to grow both in value and sophistication.

MAJOR SECTORS

DAIRY New Zealand is one of the major suppliers of dairy products in world markets, which take 90 percent of the milk produced in New Zealand. The combination of low population density, good infrastructure, and grass that grows rapidly makes New Zealand a highly competitive producer of dairy products. However, the U.S. and Western European markets strongly protect their local producers, limiting opportunities for New Zealand to penetrate these markets.

The New Zealand Dairy Board markets dairy products overseas and is one of the largest dairy companies in the world. It is seeking to develop markets in Asia and new products for North America and Western Europe. The Dairy Board is owned by the country's regional farm cooperatives. Its monopoly of exports is much debated. Although a unified and expert marketing organization offers obvious advantages to the farmers, a monopoly may also be ineffective, as a monopoly may take advantage of its total control over exports to unfairly raise prices.

Among tourists in New Zealand, the biggest spenders come from Australia, Japan, the United States, and Britain.

MEAT AND WOOL Over a quarter of New Zealand's land area is used for sheep farming. There are 10 sheep for every person, and most are dual-purpose meat and wool animals. Each year about 25 million lambs and sheep and 3 million cattle are slaughtered in New Zealand. This produces over 500 million tons (455 million metric tons) of lamb and mutton and over 500 million tons of beef and veal. New Zealand's main markets for meat are North America and the European Union.

TOURISM Tourism grew rapidly during the 1980s and 1990s, with New Zealand's isolation luring more travelers to visit, rather than deterring them. Some 1.3 million people visited New Zealand in 1995, and this number reached 2.466 million in 2007. Visitor growth has been highest from some east Asian countries, notably South Korea and Taiwan.

Tourism development requires careful handling so as not to overcrowd key sights. New attractions are continually being developed. For example, Queenstown, in the Southern Alps on Lake Wakatipu, has the style of an international ski resort, while offering ready access to wilderness walks, mountain climbing, heli-skiing, bungee-jumping, and white-water rafting (*right*), among other activities.

FORESTRY Commercial plantation forests (mainly pine) cover about 7 percent of New Zealand's land area. This is one of the largest concentrations of plantation forest and softwood in the world. New Zealand expects to supply some 39 million cubic yards (30 million cubic m) of softwood per year by 2010.

The main commercial tree species, pinus radiata, can be harvested on a 27-year cycle—the fastest of any major supplier. New Zealand accounts for a third of the world's radiata pines.

INFRASTRUCTURE New Zealand's international competitiveness and the quality of life of its population depend partly on its infrastructure. With a low population density, expenditure on roads per person is high. New Zealand relies heavily on sea transportation for overseas trade, although some high-value goods, such as flowers and seafood, are air-freighted for freshness to sophisticated markets such as Japan.

With deregulation of the ports in 1990, New Zealand's ports changed from some of the least efficient in the world to some of the most efficient, with port costs typically falling by one-half to two-thirds within two years. With the opening up of domestic air services to competition in 1987, airport and in-flight facilities improved virtually overnight.

New Zealand has the least regulated telecommunications sector in the world. Its largest supplier, Telecom, has invested heavily in new technology, and prices have fallen rapidly.

The Wairalei thermal power station. New Zealand gathers some of its electrical power from geothermal fields and hot springs, but it has no nuclear power plants.

ENVIRONMENT

NEW ZEALAND HAS ALL THE world's natural attractions packed into its two islands. One can trek on the slopes of active volcanoes, travel through remote rain forests, or even hike on glaciers, slowly making one's way toward the ocean. In the remote fjords, one can see seals and penguins, and visitors can even swim with playful dolphin pods. The adventurous can go white-water rafting or skiing down long glaciers. The pristine environment draws tourists from all over the globe.

It is not surprising that conserving the natural environment is one of the government's top priorities. New Zealand has gone so far as to set up an Environment Court to rule on decisions regarding the environment, including resource management, planning, and development matters.

ENVIRONMENTAL RECORD

If you were to tramp through New Zealand's unspoiled national parks, you would certainly appreciate the "clean and green" environment of New Zealand. The dark side of New Zealand's environmental record, however, is that three-quarters of the nation's forests have been stripped for timber and pasture over many years. Urban air pollution has risen to unprecedented levels, and introduced animals have caused havoc on the native flora and fauna.

In 1994 the government released a paper entitled *The Environment 2010 Strategy* with goals for New Zealand to achieve to justify its claim of being a clean, green country. Among the goals were protecting natural habitats and biodiversity. Some 90 percent of New Zealand's wetlands have been drained or degraded, lowland forest areas have been reduced

Above: **The environment is considered of utmost importance to many locals. Hence, signs such as these are commonly hung to fight for this cause.**

Opposite: **Mount Egmont (Taranaki) is seen in the background with New Zealand's lush greenery and beautiful lakes in the foreground.**

to 15 percent of their pre-Maori extent, and only 10 percent of the tall tussock grassland that existed in 1840 still remains. Half of New Zealand's endemic bird species have also become extinct since settlers first arrived in New Zealand. About 500 species of animals and plants are now threatened.

WILDLIFE

New Zealand's native flora and fauna are mostly endemic (they are not found anywhere else in the world). With no large native land mammals, birds dominate New Zealand's wildlife. The world's largest flightless parrot (the kakapo) and the only truly alpine parrot (the kea) are found here. The moa was driven to extinction by the arrival of humans—up to 12 feet (3.5 m) tall and weighing 440 pounds (200 kg), it was easily captured. Other species that are in peril include the kakapo and the kiwi.

The pukeko wading on top of the swampy waters of New Zealand.

KAKAPO The kakapo is an example of a bird that evolved in the absence of predators but has failed to survive in the modern competitive world. It has been described as the world's "largest, fattest, and least able to fly" parrot. It is severely endangered. A male kakapo can weigh up to 8.8 pounds (4 kg), and there are only 86 kakapos left.

PUKEKO The pukeko, or New Zealand Swamp Hen, is a member of the rail family, and is similar to other species found all over the world. It is one of the few native New Zealand birds to have flourished since the arrival of humans. It can be found in almost any grassland area, especially in swampy locations. Groups of pukeko will often be seen foraging for food in roadside areas. With their bright blue plumage and red beaks, these birds easily stand out against the New Zealand greenery.

MARINE MAMMALS

There are 76 species of whales and dolphins on Earth, and New Zealand is blessed with 35 of those species. Dolphin hotspots include the Bay of Islands in Northland and Kaikoura, north of Christchurch.

HECTOR'S DOLPHIN This dolphin is exclusive to New Zealand waters. It has a rather dumpy shape, with a distinctive rounded fin, and reaches a length of only 4.6 feet (1.4 m). Like the dusky dolphin, Hector's dolphins feed on small schooling fish, but they stay relatively close to shore year-round. The Department of Conservation (DOC) declared the Banks Peninsula (a peninsula in the Canterbury region on the east coast of the South Island of New Zealand), a marine sanctuary after Greenpeace reported that 30 percent of the Hector's dolphin population had been killed in that area. Hector's dolphin is considered the rarest species of marine dolphin, and the South Island population has been listed as "critically endangered" by the World Conservation Union (IUCN), previously known as the International Union for the Conservation of Nature and Natural Resources.

A graceful leaping dusky dolphin in Kaikoura on the South Island of New Zealand.

DUSKY DOLPHIN Dusky dolphins usually average a bit less than 6.6 feet (2 m) long, but what they lack in size they make up for in spirit. These are the most playful dolphins, and they are the kind that "dolphin swimming" participants are likely to encounter. While in the water, one may see them executing noisy leaps and somersaults. They feed on small schooling fish and often round up hundreds of fish in a tight ball, from which members of the pod take turns at feeding.

SPERM WHALES Sperm whales are the largest of the toothed whales. The male often reaches up to 66 feet (20 m) in length, while the female is much smaller, with a maximum length of 39 feet (12 m). This is the whale that watchers come to see at Kaikoura. The continental shelf (the extended area of each continent into the sea) there is so narrow that whales can be observed from the shore. Adult males weigh up to 50 tons (45,359 kg) and females weigh just over 20 tons (18,144 kg). Both live for up to 70 years. Sperm whales have a single blowhole that is offset on the left side of their head.

FLORA

New Zealand has magnificent areas of native forest. About 15 percent of its total land area is covered by native flora, much of it in protected parks and reserves.

KAURI Kauri trees grow only in the Northland and on the Coromandel Peninsula. These large native trees were once ruthlessly cut down for their excellent timber. They grow to at least 98 feet (30 m) and are believed to live for up to 2,000 years.

POHUTUKAWA This beautiful tree is predominantly found in the north part of the North Island, but it has also been successfully planted throughout the South Island. Its brilliant crimson flowers appear in December, giving it the nickname "Christmas tree." It can grow up to 66 feet (20 m) in height and 6.6 feet (2 m) across at its base, and is usually found close to the sea.

RESOURCE MANAGEMENT ACT (RMA) AND PROTECTION OF GEOTHERMAL ECOSYSTEMS

Significant geothermal features and their associated rare ecosystems occur across the Taupo Volcanic Zone, with many of the remaining outstanding geothermal features found in the Bay of Plenty Conservancy. These areas are also highly sought after for energy development.

The DOC raised concerns over a significant number of unspoiled geothermal features and ecosystems that were not provided with sufficient protection under the RMA. The department's appeal asked that the relatively pristine Te Kopia system be held as a protected system, as it holds international botanical significance and contains rare geological surface features. This suggestion was opposed by Trust Power Limited (a major electricity retailer in New Zealand), which sought development status.

The department negotiated directly with both Trust Power Limited and the regional council. In the end the company withdrew its appeal and the local government agreed to protected status for Te Kopia.

NATIONAL PARKS AND RESERVES

With the passing of the Conservation Act in 1987, the DOC was set up to protect natural and historic heritage, and to provide recreational opportunities on the land entrusted to its care. One-third of New Zealand's land has been set aside as national parks and conservation areas. The 20 million acres (8 million ha) of conservation land make an enormous contribution to regional wealth and employment, largely through tourism.

There are also many subtler and more complex economic contributions that natural environments supply, such as "ecosystem services." They are the processes that nature provides for free, from which humans benefit, such as freshwater filtration and allocation, soil maintenance, erosion and flood control, and the maintenance of food stocks. These are taken for granted because they are "free"—not traded directly in any markets—but their value to society becomes apparent when they are in decline.

ENERGY USE IN NEW ZEALAND

New Zealand currently derives its energy mainly from hydroelectric power and oil. Other significant sources of energy include coal, gas, and geothermal and thermally generated electricity. Renewable energy sources

New Zealand is home to three United Nations Educational, Scientific, and Cultural Organization (UNESCO) World Heritage Sites: Te Wahipounamu in southwest New Zealand, Tongariro National Park, and the New Zealand Sub-Antarctic Islands.

New Zealand complies with many environmental treaties, including the Kyoto Treaty (a treaty that requires industrialized nations to reduce their emissions of greenhouse gases, principally carbon dioxide) signed in 2002. Other treaties to which New Zealand is a party include the Protocol on Environmental Protection to the Antarctic Treaty and the Climate Change Declaration at the East Asia Summit.

LIST OF NATIONAL PARKS AND RESERVES

There are 14 national parks and 31 marine reserves in New Zealand.

The 14 national parks are:

Te Urewera	Paparoa
Egmont	Arthur's Pass
Whanganui	Westland/Tai Poutini
Tongariro	Aoraki/Mount Cook
Abel Tasman	Mount Aspiring
Kahurangi	Fjordland
Nelson Lakes	Rakiura

The marine reserves are:
Auckland Islands Marine Reserve
Cape Rodney-Okakari Point Marine Reserve (Goat Island)
Hawea Marine Reserve (Clio Rocks)
Horoirangi Marine Reserve
Kahukura Marine Reserve (Gold Arm)
Kapiti Marine Reserve
Kermadec Islands Marine Reserve
Kutu Parera Marine Reserve
Long Bay-Okura Marine Reserve
Long Island-Kokomohua Marine Reserve
Mayor Island Marine Reserve (Tuhua)
Moana Uta Marine Reserve
Motu Manawa-Pollen Island Marine Reserve
Parininihi Marine Reserve
Piopiotahi Marine Reserve (Milford Sound)
Pohatu Marine Reserve
Poor Knights Islands Marine Reserve
Taipari Roa Marine Reserve
Taumoana Marine Reserve
Te Angiangi Marine Reserve
Te Awaatu Channel Marine Reserve (The Gut)
Te Hapua Marine Reserve
Te Matuku Bay Marine Reserve
Te Paepae o Aotea Marine Reserve
Te Tapuwae O Hua Marine Reserve
Te Tapuwae O Rongokako Marine Reserve
Whanganui A Hei Marine Reserve (Cathedral Cove)
Tonga Island Marine Reserve
Ulva Island/Te Wharawhara Marine Reserve
Westhaven Marine Reserve (Te Tai Tapu)
Whangarei Harbor Marine Reserve

such as wind, biogas, industrial waste, and wood provide lesser amounts of energy. Since hydroelectric dams do not burn fossil fuels, they do not directly produce carbon dioxide. The cost of operating a hydroelectric plant is also immune to increases in the cost of fossil fuels, such as oil, natural gas, or coal. Reservoirs created by hydroelectric schemes often provide facilities for water sports and become tourist attractions. For instance, the Huka Falls Dam is home to the famous Huka Jet Boat, an exhilarating, once-in-a-lifetime, 30-minute water ride through the Waikato River with amazing views of the spectacular Huka Falls.

LAKE MANAPOURI Manapouri Power Station is an underground hydroelectric power station and the largest hydroelectric power station in New Zealand. It lies deep within a remote area of New Zealand's South Island on the western arm of Lake Manapouri, in Fjordland National Park. The first surveyors mapping out this corner of New Zealand noted the potential for hydrogeneration in the 584-foot (178-m) drop from the lake to the Tasman Sea at Doubtful Sound. The construction of the station was a massive feat of civil engineering. Most of the station, including the machine hall and two 6.2-mile (10-km) tailrace tunnels, was excavated under a mountain. During the 1960s environmental protests against its construction, which resulted in the planned raising of lake levels, galvanized New Zealanders, and was considered one of the starting points of New Zealand environmentalism.

The interior of the Manapouri hydropower plant in South Island of New Zealand.

A gas treatment plant in the foreground of Mount Egmont on the North Island.

NATURAL GAS IN NEW ZEALAND New Zealand uses about 163 billion cubic feet (4.5 billion cubic m) of gas each year. In 2006 oil prices rose so high that the government invited natural gas producers to send rigs to one of the most inhospitable seas on Earth—the Great South Basin off the country's southern coast. The fields below the seas south of New Zealand may contain as much as 7 trillion cubic feet (200 billion cubic m) of gas. However, the winds in this region peak at more than 93 miles (150 km) an hour and exceed 22 miles (36 km) an hour about 40 percent of the time. Some of the highest waves in the world come from this region. The potential for high reward is matched by high risk in terms of exploration costs and challenging sea and weather conditions.

CAUSES AND EFFECTS OF POLLUTION

Favorable geographic features, low population, and a late development of industry mean that New Zealand has avoided the air, water, and land pollution problems of more densely populated and heavily industrialized countries. New Zealanders are keen to take environmental responsibility on an individual, national, and international basis. Individuals and their local authorities reduce waste and recycle their trash. There are no nuclear power plants or weapons. However, there is still room for improvement in environmental management.

It is estimated that effects from air pollution occur throughout New Zealand—not just in the main cities. The primary causes include home heating, transportation in Auckland, and industry. The total economic costs are estimated to be $1.14 billion a year.

The Organization for Economic Co-operation and Development (OECD) *Environmental Performance Review of New Zealand* (2007) brought up the fact that better protection of surface water and groundwater was needed because pollution was affecting rivers, streams, and lakes. Irrigation was also taking a toll. Another area of concern was waste management. The report said that landfills should charge the full cost of disposing of waste, and that systematic tracking and treatment of hazardous waste was needed.

Smog pollution from the burning of coal and woodfires during winter in Christchurch.

A recycling center with bins for different materials in the city of Otago.

WASTE DISPOSAL AND RECYCLING

Approximately 3.8 million tons (3.4 million metric tons) of waste are dumped in New Zealand landfills every year. There has been good progress in improving waste management and waste minimization services and infrastructure across the country, and 97 percent of New Zealanders now have access to recycling facilities. Many communities have also taken the initiative to minimize waste and improve resource recovery.

CLIMATE CHANGE

New Zealand is unique when compared with other developed countries, because half of its emissions come from the agricultural sector. The nation produces less than 0.5 percent of global greenhouse gas emissions, but because of the methane emitted from ruminant animals, New Zealand's emissions are the 11th highest in the world on a per capita basis, despite the fact that much more than half of the electricity produced already comes from renewable sources.

The biologically based economy is particularly vulnerable to a changing and unstable climate. The snow cover in the ski areas is expected to decrease, and there will be a shortened season of snowfall. Also, the glaciers are expected to reduce in ice volume and length. The sea level is expected to go up, and the strongest increases in temperature will occur in winter. Most important, climate change is expected to bring more droughts to areas that are already prone to drought, and more floods are expected in those areas that are already vulnerable to flood. The last major drought, in 1997 to 1998, cost the economy a billion dollars, and the floods of February 2004 are estimated to have cost well over $300 million. New Zealand's energy base is aso heavily dependent on the climate, as hydroelectric power generates about 67 percent of electrical energy.

To adapt to the economic and social impacts of climate change, New Zealand's government has established a strong agricultural research program and is introducing an adaptation program. Hopefully the work of the government will enable Kiwis (people who are native to New Zealand) to reduce risks and increase opportunities from the unavoidable impacts of climate change.

PESTS IN NEW ZEALAND

The Australian brush-tailed possum was introduced into New Zealand in 1837 to establish a fur trade. Today there are 70 million of them roaming the country, eating native bush and threatening endangered animals such as giant land snails and kiwi. Stoats and rats also threaten native birds. Efforts to eradicate them have included the use of the biodegradable pesticide 1080 (sodium fluoroacetate). The DOC has also introduced mainland "islands," which are manageable areas isolated by means of fencing or geographical features. Through intensive management of these islands, the DOC hopes to cultivate them as a way to protect and restore habitats on the mainland by eradicating all pests as thoroughly as possible.

NEW ZEALANDERS

DURING THE FIRST 50 YEARS of European settlement (between 1831 and 1881), the European population of New Zealand increased from fewer than 1,000 people to half a million. In 1886, 40 percent of these Europeans were British, coming from England, Scotland, Wales, and Ireland. They came mostly from working-class and lower-middle-class backgrounds. It was the intention of the New Zealand Company and the government to people New Zealand with Britons—to create a "Britain of the South." Over 150 years later New Zealand is a kaleidoscope of different peoples from Asia, Polynesia, and many other parts of the world.

TOILS AND TITLES

New Zealand was oversold in Britain as a "Land of Promise" with very fertile soil, banana plantations, and other tropical fruit orchards. Steep hillsides covered in bush and scrub were described as "perfect for grapevines, wheat, and olives." A few aristocrats also moved to New Zealand, hoping to establish themselves as the elite of the new society. Many returned to Europe, finding life in New Zealand too tough. Nonetheless the trappings of success from Europe soon arrived in New Zealand—large houses, servants, balls, fine clothes, and etiquette.

It was not long before the British government conferred honors on residents of the colony, such as "knights" and the female equivalent, "dames." Today New Zealand has its own honors system—a reflection of the confidence that New Zealanders have as a nation that stands apart from Britain.

Above: **New Zealand's cosmopolitan population can be seen through this group of youths in the Parakai Springs Aquatic Park in Auckland.**

Opposite: **A smiling young girl carries a baby lamb.**

European immigrants to New Zealand: a family with Dutch ancestry.

OTHER MIGRANTS

Migrants came also from Australia (mainly whalers and sealers, but also escaped convicts), France, Germany, Scandinavia, Dalmatia, Lebanon, Southern Europe, and Asia. As with the Australians, some of the American whalers and sealers also decided to make New Zealand their base. The Chinese came out to work in the gold fields of Central Otago in the 1860s and 1870s (as did many Australians), and a large influx of Dutch migrants poured into the country after World War II.

Nestling on the slopes of pristine pastureland by the calm waters of Banks Peninsula (near Christchurch) is the historic French settlement of Akaroa. French street names and stone buildings with shutters preserve its Gallic heritage. The main street, Rue Lavaud, commemorates French seaman Charles Lavaud, who captained the warship *L'Aube* that escorted Captain Jean Langlois's party of 63 immigrants from Rochefort in 1840. The Treaty of Waitangi and consequent British sovereignty over New Zealand ended Langlois's dreams of a French colony, but his settlers stayed on.

AN INTREPID EXPLORER

The topography of New Zealand made travel difficult for early settlers. A young Englishman named Thomas Brunner set out on foot in 1846 to seek a pass across the Southern Alps. For 18 months, in the company of two Maori, he explored previously untrodden forested mountains. Often close to starvation, he subsisted on fern roots and eventually had to eat his dog. He risked his life crossing dangerous rivers, and when his boots were finally torn to pieces, his Maori companions made him sandals from flax and the leaves of the cabbage tree. Before his great journey was over, Brunner fell ill (and lost the use of one leg). While he was sheltering under an overhanging rock one night, all of the precious sketches and notebooks that he kept in a flax basket fell into his campfire and were burned. Still he did not lose heart, and he completed his successful expedition long after he had been given up for dead.

MOTHERLAND

Most New Zealanders are descendants of the early European settlers, mainly from Britain. Until fairly recently Britain was considered the motherland of most New Zealanders, with thousands of people making pilgrimages home to the "old country" every year. Today large numbers of people still visit Britain and Europe, but their purpose is more to experience life in another country than to rediscover their ancestral roots.

TOUGH BEGINNINGS

Unlike early North American settlements, most New Zealand settlers did not come to New Zealand for political or religious reasons. Instead they came with the common goal of getting ahead in life, owning and establishing their own farms and small businesses. This common purpose was, to some extent, reflected in the motto of the first New Zealand coat of arms (an official symbol of New Zealand), which read "Onward." But the land was not as fertile as the earlier settlers had been led to believe, and a lot of hard work was needed to clear thick bush before farms could be established.

A New Zealander of British descent. Life was hard for many of these early settlers.

PIONEERING SPIRIT

In adapting to their new environment, the early settlers had to make many compromises and improvisations. This has affected the way New Zealanders think of themselves today. "Kiwi ingenuity" is a common expression that epitomizes the positive attitude of New Zealanders when it comes to difficult or challenging situations, often involving the use of ordinary things to achieve extraordinary results. The stories of Richard Pearse, William Hamilton, and John Britten illustrate this New Zealand pioneering spirit.

Aviation Pioneer

Richard Pearse (1877–1953) was a Canterbury farmer who began the construction of his first aircraft in the late 19th century. He worked alone and without any financial backing. His aircraft had a bamboo and aluminum frame (made from flattened-out sheep-dip tins—large tins containing preparations of liquid disinfectant into which sheep are dipped to destroy parasites and to clean their wool, especially before shearing) braced with wire—a high-wing monoplane mounted on bicycle wheels with a span of about 26 feet (8 m). It was powered by a two-cylinder engine, which Pearse built himself.

   According to witnesses, he flew his aircraft for about 0.6 mile (1 km) on March 31, 1903, months before the famous Wright brothers made their first flight in America. Unlike the American brothers, however, Pearse did not go on to perfect his aircraft.

The First Jet Boat

William Hamilton (1899–1978) was a South Canterbury farmer and amateur engineer who developed and perfected the principle of water-jet propulsion to drive propellerless boats in the 1950s. By the 1960s there was a huge international demand for his commercial units. Hamilton's jet units are high-pressure water pumps driven by adapted car engines. Hamilton jet boats are now used on the Colorado River.

The Cardinal Britten Superbike

In little more than a garden shed, the late John Britten (1950–1995), a Christchurch design engineer, toiled to design and build the fastest four-stroke (an internal-combustion engine with a cycle of four strokes—intake, compression, combustion, and exhaust) motorcycle in the world, the Cardinal Britten V1000. This innovative bike has aerodynamics that are unequaled by other motorcycles and breathtaking sleekness. At its widest point the Britten's engine is no thicker than the rear tire.

   Britten's achievement was quite remarkable. European and American motorcycle magazine writers heaped praise on the Britten V1000 bike after it won the International Battle of the Twins (two-cylinder bikes) at Assen, Holland, in 1992.

   For John Britten, designing bikes started out as a hobby. He also wanted to prove "that there is room for the individual to compete against the multimillion-dollar factory jobs." Now replicas of the Cardinal Brittens are being built for overseas collectors.

TWO SOCIETIES—MAORI AND PAKEHA

As Anglo-Saxons became predominant in the community, Maori people, who had been dominant in 1840, became subordinate to the Europeans by 1890. Two societies existed in New Zealand, although there was considerable racial interaction between them, including some intermarriages between the Maori and Europeans. Separate schools for Maori and Pakeha had the aim of preparing Maori for life among their own people and for Europeans to be trained in the professions, trade, and commerce. The Maori retained their traditional social structures and ceremonies, such as the *hui* (hoo-ee), a political and a social gathering to which Europeans were often invited. Likewise Europeans invited Maori chiefs to their balls and civic dinners.

By the early 1950s the Maori population had recovered substantially in number, but they had lost control of a significant portion of their land during the land wars of the late 19th century. A shift from the rural areas to the towns and cities began, and by 1956 nearly a quarter of the Maori population were urban dwellers.

A female laundry worker. Educated mainly in agriculture, metalworking, home management, and cooking, Maori migrants to the cities found work in the factories, the building trades, and laboring occupations.

With the continuing urbanization of the Maori, intermarriage with the Pakeha increased. However, Maori people did not totally assimilate into the Pakeha culture. Instead, they took positive steps to maintain their own way of life.

URBANIZATION OF MAORI

Various programs, including housing assistance, were established to help the Maori, especially the younger generation, adapt to urban living and integrate into mainstream Pakeha society. In the rural areas the Maori social structure follows the kinship networks of *whanau* (FAA-no-oo), or extended family; *hapu* (huh-POO), or subtribe; and *iwi* (ee-wee), or tribe. Within each tribe there is a clearly defined system of rank and social control consisting of male and female elders, parents, uncles and aunts, religious mentors, and Maori wardens. When the Maori youth stepped out of these constraints—for instance, by moving to the cities from their tribal location—many of them discovered that they lacked the ability to manage their freedom, and soon fell into conflict with the law. Sadly, even today, there is a much higher proportion of Maori offenders in New Zealand prisons than Pakeha.

A serious attempt was made through the support of voluntary associations (including churches and cultural and sports clubs) to help the Maori retain their cultural identity and spiritual values. Central to rural Maori life is the *marae* (mah-rye) with its ancestral house, where both religious and secular activities take place. Eventually city *marae* were established. Today there are even *marae* facilities on the campuses of secondary schools, colleges, and universities. However, for special occasions, such as weddings, Maori people journey back to their traditional tribal areas, to the *marae* where their ancestors debated important tribal decisions for generations.

MAORI ACTIVISTS

As they moved to the towns and cities, the Maori people learned much about the Pakeha political and social systems that governed their lives, and they began to use radical and activist means to gain equality and social justice and a return of their assets, such as land and fisheries. Land became the symbol of Maori political subjection to Pakeha laws and was a sensitive issue in the central government.

Today the Maori people represent 15 percent of the total population of New Zealand, and they are enjoying a cultural renaissance that continues to strengthen. They have their own television channel called Maori Television and many radio stations, which meet the needs of their communities. They now have a bigger representation than previously in Parliament. The independent Maori Congress is a forum for tribes to come together to discuss important matters, and the Maori Council promotes the social and economic well-being of the Maori people and Maori culture. The council has won several court cases concerning land claims against the New Zealand government.

By the 1970s, when 75 percent of the Maori population had become urbanized, there was a move to preserve Maori culture through clubs teaching Maori action songs, oratory, arts and crafts, and *marae* etiquette.

Somalians are among the many nationalities who have been attracted to the New Zealand lifestyle.

REFUGEES

New Zealand has one of the world's highest intakes of refugees per head of population. Refugees from Europe arrived in the 1930s and again after World War II. Many of these were Jews and Poles. Following the 1956 Hungarian uprising, there was an influx of refugees from Hungary.

The Communist victory and takeover of South Vietnam also resulted in an exodus of refugees. Since 1975 about 7,000 Indochinese refugees have been resettled in New Zealand. Other refugees include Chileans, Russian Jews, Eastern Europeans, Assyrians, and, more recently, Cambodians and Iraqis.

PACIFIC ISLANDERS

The fourth-largest ethnic group in New Zealand is the Pacific Island Polynesians, whose members make up 6 percent of the total population and are based largely in the Auckland area. Today Auckland is the largest Polynesian city in the world, and small countries, such as Niue and Tokelau, have more of their people in New Zealand than they do at home. The Pacific Islanders have been flowing into New Zealand since the early 1960s, mainly for economic reasons. Young people from Pacific islands such as Western Samoa, Tonga, the Cook Islands, Niue, and Fiji have a greater potential for receiving a better education and finding employment in New Zealand than in their country of origin. A Ministry of

Pacific Island Affairs ensures that the specific needs of the Pacific Islanders are met—for instance, for skills training and employment placement service—while at the same time recognizing the cultural values and aspirations of the Islanders.

ASIANS

Since the 1980s an increasing number of Asian migrants have been coming to New Zealand. These include people from Taiwan, South Korea, Hong Kong, and mainland China. The Indian population is the fastest growing of the Asian populations in the country, and a corner "dairy" run by an Indian family is an institution.

The increasingly multicultural character of New Zealand has meant that Kiwi society has grown increasingly cosmopolitan and vibrant. No longer restricted to Maori and Pakeha, each ethnic group contributes its own customs, culture, and influences to the New Zealand lifestyle.

AGING POPULATION

Compared with most developed Western countries, New Zealand has always had a young population because of the large-scale immigration of mainly young adults and a high birthrate during the 20th century. However, it has been predicted that New Zealand's population will grow more slowly in the future—by less than 1 percent a year, with the elderly population being the fastest-growing age group.

An elderly lady poses with her daughter. New Zealanders enjoy one of the world's highest life expectancy rates—82.3 years for females and 78.3 years for males.

71

LIFESTYLE

THERE USED TO BE A COMMONLY used phrase among New Zealanders that described their basic attitude toward life—"She'll be right, mate." (It is the attitude that the situation, repairs, or whatever has been done is adequate or sufficient for what is needed. This is often perceived as carelessness, especially when a failure occurs.) There is less complacency today, but there remains a sense of optimism. New Zealanders are positive about being New Zealanders.

FAMILY LIFE

Family life in New Zealand is changing. Although the traditional nuclear family still predominates, there are now de facto couple families, single-parent families, and a few homosexual couple families. The divorce rate is increasing, but so, too, is the number of people who remarry. This often results in the blending of two families. Women are having children later in life. Many couples choose not to have children, and those who do have fewer kids; one-child families are now the most common kind.

Left: **A typical family unit in New Zealand. Many families are now opting for fewer children.**

Opposite: **People dining outdoors in the New Regent Street Mall in Christchurch. Most locals enjoy catching up with friends or family in cafés such as these.**

A Maori family enjoying a picnic. For the matriarchal Maori society, the *whanau*, or extended family, may include three or four generations. Traditionally, the *whanau* provided food and shelter, and cared for the land. Even in contemporary society, it is still common to have members of the extended family living together.

ON THE MARAE

The Maori believe that a *marae* is their "standing place," a place where, as a family, they know they belong—it is, in a sense, their "home." The *marae* is a social place of hospitality where food and shelter are offered, but it is also a place of strict protocol. Women have a special role on the *marae*. Visitors assemble outside its gates and await the *karanga* (kah-rah-ngah), or call to enter, which is always made by a woman. A female leader returns the *karanga* on behalf of the visitors. She then leads the visitors in a slow procession onto the *marae*, calling as she goes.

Very important visitors to a *marae* are ceremonially challenged—in other words, they first need to go through a ceremony called *Te Wero* in which the challenger (always a man) makes fierce faces and noises, swinging a *taiaha* (tye-aha), or spearlike weapon, at the visitors to show that the warriors are ready to defend themselves if necessary. A small carved challenge dart is placed on the ground before the visitors, and is always picked up by a male visitor. This indicates that the visitors arrive in peace. Traditionally this was done to establish whether visitors came in war or in peace.

Once visitors are in front of the meeting house, a *powhiri* (POR-fi-ree), or welcome, is given by elders, both men and women. The *powhiri* serves to ward off evil spirits, keeping visitors safe as they move onto the *marae*. Those who take part in the powhiri are protected by the *tapu* (tuh-poo) of the *marae*. *Tapu* is a purely Maori word that is associated with Maori spiritual beliefs. It means "sacred" or "holy." When the Maori people declare something to be *tapu*—for example, the ground on a *marae*—then it is necessary to approach this area according to prescribed ritual. Many Maori believe that ignoring *tapu* will bring sickness or even death.

After the welcome speeches are made, women sing a *waiata* (wye-uh-tah), or song. The last visitor to speak lays a *koha* (kor-hah), or gift, on the ground. Today the *koha* will often be money, but tribes used to give food. When all the speeches are over the visitors can greet the hosts with a *hongi* (hor-ngee). A *hongi* is a traditional greeting of the Maori people. The pressing of noses during the *hongi* mingles the breath of two people in a show of unity.

EDUCATION

Schooling is compulsory from age six to 16, but nearly all children begin school at age five, and many continue until the age of 18. The government partially funds an array of early-childhood service providers, all of whom are independent of the government; these include play centers, kindergartens, and Maori language tests. After three years at secondary school most pupils take the National Certificate of Educational Achievement exams. Students work to achieve credits that will count toward their qualifications when they leave school and their university entrance criteria.

Private schools are partially funded by the government and charge student fees to cover their costs. Privately owned schools can also be integrated into the public system and receive funding. Integration has mostly been used by Catholic schools, some of which successfully serve the poorest areas in the cities. About 8 percent of students attend integrated schools, and 3 percent attend private, fee-charging schools.

Educational achievement by the Maori people has not kept pace with that of other groups, but alternate programs are being studied and

The focal point of the *marae* is the meeting house or *whare* (wuh-re), the shape of which is believed to represent the ancestor's body. A carved figure on the rooftop represents the head of the ancestor, while carved sloping pieces are the arms. Inside, a central ridge pole is the backbone and the rafters are the ribs. Large poles support the ridge pole and represent the link between the Sky Father and the Earth Mother.

tribes are being given assistance to develop their own educational plans. A limited number of schools that teach mainly in the Maori language are funded within the state system.

The Correspondence School (a school that teaches nonresident students by mail) is a world leader in distance education. It provides courses from early childhood to adult part-time students who wish to continue their basic education. Many students in isolated rural areas receive their education through the Correspondence School.

New Zealand has eight universities, with around 100,000 students. All of the universities are publicly owned but run by independent councils. There are also some 20 publicly owned polytechnic schools that teach mostly lower-level courses, although some also issue university degrees. About 100,000 students attend the polytechnics. There are three colleges of education that offer courses in teacher training. New Zealand's secondary schools, polytechnics, and universities accept many tuition-paying foreign students.

THE WORKPLACE

There are now about as many women employed in the professions of law, medicine, and accounting as there are men. There is equal pay for equal work, but not always equal opportunity.

The old arts building and clocktower at the University of Auckland.

Many young people leave home around the age of 20 and live in apartments with their peers. This is often necessary in order to be near their place of work—particularly for those growing up in rural areas. Over half of those commuting to work go by car; less than 5 percent travel by bus or rail.

CITY LIFE

New Zealand cities are not places where heavy industry dominates the skyline. Modern high-rise office buildings specially designed to withstand earthquakes rub shoulders with sculptured buildings of interesting design and 100-year-old pubs.

The area around Wellington, for example, has often been rocked by earthquakes. The city sits on a major earthquake fault line. Many of the city's older buildings have been replaced by buildings that are specially constructed to withstand severe quakes. As a result Wellington boasts the most modern skyline of any city in New Zealand.

Auckland, Wellington, and Christchurch are cities of wide ethnic diversity and culture. This is seen in the huge variety of restaurants, street cafés, and colorful street markets.

Shopping malls provide convenient one-stop shopping and places in which to stroll. Large supermarkets have displaced many small grocers and butchers, but the local dairy continues. Usually managed by Indian families and open until late in the evening, these small corner shops crammed with dairy (convenience store) products, ice cream, cakes, candy, flowers, and magazines are still in demand.

Although inner-city apartments are becoming popular, most city-dwellers still reside in spacious houses with gardens in the surrounding suburbs. The economic divide is not as marked as, for example, that of New York, but the gap between the rich and the less well-off is evident, particularly in parts of Auckland where there are large pockets of poorer Maori and Pacific Islanders.

Because it was found to be expensive and difficult to fertilize undulating or very hilly farmland by hand or with vehicles, in 1926 a Hunterville farmer named John Lambert promoted the idea of using small planes from which to drop fertilizers. This is believed to be the first use of aerial topdressing (the spreading of fertilizers over farmland by means of aircraft) in the world.

77

ERNEST RUTHERFORD: ATOM MAN (1871–1937)

Ernest Rutherford was one of the greatest scientists of the 20th century and a forerunner of the nuclear age. He was born in Brightwater, near Nelson, New Zealand, in 1871. Rutherford received his early education in government schools, and at the age of 16, he entered Nelson Collegiate School. In 1889 he was awarded a university scholarship and proceeded to the University of New Zealand, Wellington, where he entered Canterbury College. He graduated with a master's degree in 1893 with a double major in mathematics and physical science. He continued with research work at the college for a short time, receiving a bachelor of science degree the following year (he earned his bachelor's undergraduate degree so that he could apply for the Exhibition Science Scholarhip that would enable him to take up research anywhere in the world). That same year, 1894, he was awarded an Exhibition Science Scholarship, enabling him to go to Trinity College, Cambridge, as a research student at the Cavendish Laboratory under J. J. Thomson. In 1898 he moved to McGill University in Montreal, where he held the position of professor of physics. Rutherford returned to Cambridge's Cavendish Laboratory as director, in 1919, and became well known for having a personality that matched his achievements, mentoring and directing others toward great discoveries. He was awarded the Nobel Prize in Chemistry for his investigations into the disintegration of the elements and the chemistry of radioactive substances in 1908 and a baronetcy in 1931, choosing the title Baron Rutherford of Nelson and choosing as his coat of arms a design that included a kiwi and a Maori warrior. He has been featured on stamps in New Zealand, Sweden, Russia, and Canada. He remained proud of his New Zealand origins and his family. After his death in 1937, his medals were gifted to Canterbury College, now the University of Canterbury. In 1992 his image was placed on the new New Zealand $100 bill.

Poorer neighborhoods in New Zealand are dominated by individual low-rise state housing. The facilities are adequate, although the neighborhoods are rougher and the schools less desirable.

RURAL LIFE

Life in the countryside and the small towns is community-driven. Entertainment is less passive than in the cities—country people have to

A rural piece of farmland on Urupukapuka in New Zealand.

create their own fun, and they are very good at it. Social activities revolve around clubs, the local church, the local pub, and the *marae.*

The community hall is a focus for important birthdays such as a 21st, which is still celebrated in style. There are country balls, barn dances, musicals, and plays. There are also agricultural fairs, craft shows, flower shows, shearing competitions, and many other activities.

New Zealand farms are highly efficient. Unlike farms in some other countries, they are not heavily subsidized. There are 80,000 farms in New Zealand, the largest of which is 444,000 acres (180,000 ha); the average farm size is 610 acres (250 ha). Farms range from those that raise livestock, such as sheep, dairy cattle, and deer, to those involved in intensive horticulture, growing wheat, oats, barley, corn, linseed, and potatoes.

Farmers also grow fodder crops to feed their herds. There are farms that specialize in citrus fruit, kiwifruit, hops, tobacco, avocados, and many other fruits.

Among those who live in remote areas such as the high country sheep stations that nestle under the Southern Alps, the whole family is involved in tending the animals and crops. Children receive their education through the Correspondence School. Many go on to attend a boarding school in the cities for their secondary and vocational education. Not all young people return to work at the family farm.

Helicopters are used extensively today to spray insecticides over crops, to drop poisons to rid noxious animals, and to bring fencing and other supplies into an inaccessible country. There are more helicopters used in New Zealand per capita than anywhere else in the world.

WEDDINGS

Many people choose to have their wedding in a church (including Maori people, whose church is usually located on the *marae*). Others have a simple ceremony in the office of a registrar. Contemporary young couples sometimes select a more unusual location, such as a snow-covered mountain top or a sandy beach.

Nowadays there is no set format for the wedding service—couples can decide for themselves how they want to express their vows to one another. Another break with tradition often occurs at the wedding reception that follows the service, when the bride chooses to be one of the speechmakers. Taking photographs is a very important part of the wedding. Couples choose a variety of backgrounds, both unusual and traditional. After the photography

FOOTROT FLATS

Murray Ball created "Footrot Flats" and its celebrated inhabitants, Wal and Dog, in the mid-1970s. The famous cartoon strip is a self-mocking portrayal of a New Zealander character who is hardworking and unassertive. The stories, involving a man, his dog, and sheep, have been translated into a successful stage musical, a cartoon feature film, and many books.

session, the feast, the cutting of the wedding cake, speeches, and often a dance, the newlyweds depart on their honeymoon. If the couple can afford it this might be a romantic holiday on a Pacific island.

FUNERALS

The Maori believe that a body should not be left on its own after death. The family will usually collect the body from the undertaker and place it on the *marae*, where it can be watched over by relatives and friends until burial. To help relieve their emotional pain, Maori will often leave the coffin open so they can touch the body and weep over it. At the funeral service speeches are made directly to the body in the belief that the spirit does not leave the presence of the body until the burial. Some Pakeha also bring the body home from the undertaker for two or three days before burial. Others prefer to visit the body at the mortuary in the days leading up to the funeral. A funeral service is usually held in a church of the deceased's religious denomination or in the undertaker's chapel. Hymns are sung, prayers are offered, and eulogies are given by relatives and close friends. The body is then either cremated or buried in a graveyard, which is usually located just outside the town or city.

Pallbearers carrying the Maori queen, Dame Te Atairangikaahu toward the Taupiri Cemetery in Waikato during her funeral.

81

RELIGION

CHRISTIANITY PLAYED A MAJOR PART in the early colonization of New Zealand. Before the white missionaries arrived in 1814, the Maori were a fiercely competitive tribal people with no written language. They worshipped their own gods and goddesses. Through their Christian teaching the missionaries encouraged the Maori people to live together peacefully, and transformed an intelligent but illiterate people into a literate society.

The main religion in New Zealand today is still Christianity. There are also Hindus, Buddhists, and Jews. Unlike in some European countries, such as Germany, no direct state aid is given to any form of religion.

MAORI MYTHOLOGY

Traditional Maori mythology gave meaning to the supernatural and to nature. The primal myth "Origins" tells of a supreme god named Io, who brought into being the heavens, the Earth, and other gods—notably Io's Sky Father, Rangi, and Earth Mother, Papa, who produced 70 offspring, including man. Woman, however, was created by many gods.

Tane, god of the forests, shaped woman's body from clay, and her eyes were set into pieces of clouds (to make the whites of her eyes). The god of winds gave her lungs and another god plucked feathers from birds to make her hair. Tumatauenga, the god of war, arranged the muscles of her body, and Rongo, the god of peace, gave her a stomach. Her spirit, blood, and power to breathe were supplied by Io.

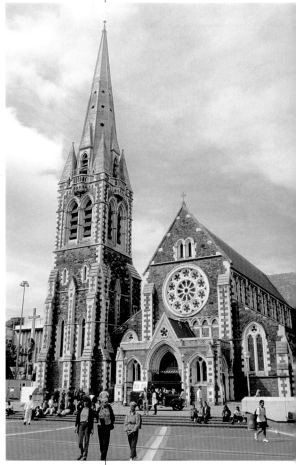

Above and opposite: **The interior (*opposite*) and exterior (*above*) of the famous Christchurch Cathedral.**

Another myth tells of the demigod Maui, who hauled the North Island out of the sea with a chip of his grandmother's jawbone (which was supposed to have magical powers) attached to his fishhook. Once his canoe was resting high and dry on the back of the "fish" (the North Island of New Zealand), Maui went off to make an offering to the gods.

While he was gone, his brothers began to cut up the "fish" to eat it. This is how the cliffs, valleys, plains, and mountain ranges of the North Island were formed.

THE WRITTEN WORD

The Protestant missionaries (Anglicans) were the first to arrive in New Zealand. By 1819 they had established two mission stations in the Bay of Islands in the North Island. The Roman Catholics and Wesleyans (Methodists) arrived a few years later.

To reach out to the Maori, the Anglicans set up a printing press and began publishing portions of the Bible in the Maori language. These biblical texts became the textbook from which the Maori learned to read and write.

An engraving of Christ wearing a Maori cloak. Images like these encouraged the spread of Christianity among the Maori people.

Maori people were quick to recognize the advantages of Christianity and literacy. There was also enhancement of *mana*, or prestige, to be gained by the tribal chiefs, who became patrons and protectors of missionaries, "the bearers of knowledge." Christianity spread very quickly among the Maori people, who became enthusiastic evangelists, often reaching new areas with the Bible ahead of the European missionaries.

LOST TRIBE OF ISRAEL?

Culturally the Maori began to identify themselves with biblical stories. Through their appreciation of an oral history and the delineation of genealogies, or ancestral descent, some Maori supposedly "discovered" their genealogical roots in Judaism, calling themselves *Hurai*, or Jews. Until the Pakeha came, the Maori people did not have a name for themselves. It is thought that seeing themselves as a lost tribe of Israel gave some Maori a new sense of cultural identity.

A number of prophetic movements grew out of the newfound religion. Maori chiefs were inspired by Old Testament (the first section of the two-part Christian Bible) prophets and leaders, who were empowered by a God who communicated with them and helped them.

As more and more Maori became literate, they began to interpret the Bible for themselves, and many forms of Maori Christianity emerged. Some forms retained the Maori notion of *tapu*, with its associated rituals.

Toward the end of the 19th century there was more uniformity within Maoridom. In a way Christianity became a unifying force between the Maori and Pakeha, but the Maori were very much subordinate.

The richly decorated interior of a Maori church.

RELIGION TODAY

Although Christianity remains the main religion, an increasing number of New Zealanders claim to have no religion at all. Less than 20 percent of the population are actively involved in churches. Among the

THE RATANA MOVEMENT

Tahupotiki Wiremu Ratana was an ordinary Maori with an unusual mission. He believed that God had called him to unify the Maori people as God's chosen race—identifying them with the Israelites as previous prophets had done. Bill Ratana, as he was known, rejected many traditional practices, such as tribalism and *tapu*, and encouraged practical pursuits such as wheat farming. He practiced faith healing all over the country. This was at a time—1918—when a major flu epidemic had seriously affected the Maori people. The population of the Maori was at an all-time low around at the beginning of the 20th century, due, in large part, to their lack of resistance to European diseases.

Ratana's influence among the Maori increased, and in 1931, in a loose alliance with the Labour Party, the Ratana Church won its first Maori seat in Parliament, going on to strongly influence Maori national politics. Today the Ratana Church is one of the fastest growing religions in New Zealand.

TARORE'S STORY

This is a true story. One day Tarore and her people embarked on a long journey to avoid persecution by a rival tribe. They set out for a place of safety in the Bay of Plenty on the North Island. On the way they camped overnight. As they settled down to sleep, the group was unaware that five raiders from a tribe in Rotorua were watching them.

In the early hours of the morning, the raiders stole many items from the camp. One warrior, called Uita, noticed that Tarore was clutching a flax bag, which contained her precious copy of one of the books in the Bible. Tarore had been given a Maori translation of the Gospel of Luke (one of the four Gospels in the New Testament that contain details of Jesus's birth and preachings) by a missionary, after she attended a mission school where she learned to read her language. Tarore refused to let go of her flax bag, and Uita, determined to get it because he thought it must contain something valuable, killed her during the struggle.

When Uita and his group returned to Rotorua with their loot, they met a young man called Ripahau. Ripahau was able to read the Maori language. He read to them from Tarore's Gospel of Luke. The story told of how God reached down in love to his creation by sending his son, Jesus Christ, to bridge the gap between God and humankind. He also read about how Jesus healed the sick, preached a gospel of peace, sacrificed his life by dying on a cross to redeem everyone from their sins, and rose again to return to heaven. The lives of everyone who listened were challenged, and some were changed.

Ripahau himself became a Christian. A short while later he traveled to Kapiti Island, situated just off the southwest coast of the North Island. There he shared the word of God with Tamihana, the son of the great Maori chief Te Rauparaha, as well as Tamihana's cousins. The cousins were so impressed with the words of Luke's Gospel that they got into their canoes and traveled to the South Island, where they spent 18 months sharing the Gospel story. Many tribespeople converted to Christianity. Young Tarore had died, but her little book had traveled on.

Christians in New Zealand, the Roman Catholics, Anglicans, Presbyterians, Pentecostals, and Baptists have the biggest percentage of followers. Other groups include Methodists, Lutherans, Brethren, the Salvation Army, Seventh-Day Adventists, and Orthodox Christians.

Pentecostal churches are now the fastest growing. The Pentecostal Church emerged from revivals in Wales and the United States in the early 20th century. During the 1960s and 1970s a charismatic renewal movement swept through the mainstream churches, softening denominational barriers and bringing refreshing new worship music. New Pentecostal churches, with multicultural and youthful congregations, were founded during this time. Some churchgoers anticipate another revival. The form of Christian church services ranges from the very traditional (found in some Roman Catholic and Anglican churches), with full choirs and organ accompaniment, chants, formal prayers, and ritualistic observances, to a freer, more informal kind (seen in the evangelical and Pentecostal churches), with contemporary music and spontaneous singing by the congregation.

A Christian radio station, pioneered 20 years ago in a shed in someone's backyard in Christchurch, now broadcasts seven days a week, 24 hours a day, throughout the nation. It features lively, contemporary Christian music and bands from Australia, the United States, and New Zealand. As the first successful Christian radio network, it has been used as a model by other countries.

Catholics attending a Mass held at Saint Patrick's Cathedral in Auckland.

87

Christian hymn singers standing next to a painting of Christ in the Polynesian Market in Wellington.

BREAKING DOWN BARRIERS

The first World Christian Gathering of Indigenous Peoples was held in Rotorua in 1996. Chaired by Monty Ohia, a prominent Maori educator, the conference drew together indigenous groups from around the globe, including American Indians, Australian Aborigines, and black South Africans.

The aim of the international conference was to build bridges between cultures and to encourage individual groups to retain their cultural distinctiveness within a Christian framework. Christianity has truly come a long way from the early missionaries' view that to become fully Christianized, people had to subordinate their own culture to that of the missionaries.

TODAY'S MISSIONS

New Zealand has the highest number of missionaries per capita in the Western world. As a nation, the people of New Zealand give generously to charitable causes such as World Vision (an international Christian relief and development organization) and Feed the Hungry (an organization dedicated to fighting world hunger). Food banks run by volunteers and many other missions of compassion minister to the needy.

GOD'S OWN COUNTRY

Thomas Bracken, a 19th-century English poet, was so impressed with the lavish beauty of New Zealand that he wrote a poem about it, calling it "God's Own Country." It is often referred to now with a touch of irony as "Godzone."

Bracken wrote another poem entitled "God Defend New Zealand," which was set to music by John J. Woods and is now one of New Zealand's two national anthems. "God Defend New Zealand" was given equal status with the traditional British anthem, "God Save the Queen," in 1977 as a mark of New Zealand's identity.

The following are the first two of the five verses of "God Defend New Zealand," in both English and Maori.

"God Defend New Zealand"	*"Aotearoa"*
God of nations at Thy feet	*E Ihoa Atua,*
In the bonds of love we meet.	*O nga Iwi! Matoura,*
Hear our voices, we entreat,	*Ata whakarongona;*
God defend our free land.	*Me aroha roa.*
Guard Pacific's triple star	*Kia hua ko te pai;*
From the shafts of strife and war,	*Kia tau to atawhai;*
Make her praises heard afar,	*Manaakitia mai*
God defend New Zealand.	*Aotearoa.*
Men of every creed and race	*Ona mano tangata*
Gather here before Thy face,	*Kiri whereo, kiri ma,*
Asking Thee to bless this place,	*Iwi Maori Pakeha*
God defend our free land.	*Repeke katoa,*
From dissension, envy, hate,	*Nei ka tono ko nga*
And corruption, guard our state,	*Mau e whakaahu ke,*
Make our country good and great,	*Kia ora marire*
God defend New Zealand.	*Aotearoa.*

LANGUAGE

ENGLISH, THE OFFICIAL LANGUAGE of New Zealand, was inherited from the early British colonizers. English is the first language of about 95 percent of the population and the only language spoken by some 90 percent, making New Zealand one of the most monolingual nations in the world.

Since 1987 Maori has also become an official language. After years of decline, there is now renewed interest in Maori, especially among the young, both Maori and non-Maori. New Zealand Sign Language, the main language of the deaf community in New Zealand, also became an official language of New Zealand in April 2006.

NEW ZEALAND GRAMMAR

People in New Zealand are educated in Standard British English. In fact New Zealand English is more like British English than any other non-European variety. The national newspapers and public documents are written in Standard English. Nevertheless Maori words have found their way into the vocabulary, and the language has been influenced by both Australian and American English.

When they are overseas New Zealanders are often mistaken for Australians, but to a New Zealand ear, the Australian accent sounds quite different—just as a Canadian accent is noticeable to an American. The main difference concerns the short "i" vowel. The Australian term *fish and chips* sounds like "feesh and cheeps" to a New Zealander, who would pronounce it "fush and chups," and *Sydney* sounds like "Seedney." However, the practice of turning a statement into what seems like a question—what phonetic experts call high rising terminal intonation—is common to both.

Above: **A woman communicating in sign language, which is now recognized as one of the official languages of New Zealand.**

Opposite: **A sign post in Waikato, in the North Island.**

A group of friends chatting in a park.

PRONUNCIATION

New Zealand pronunciation departs from Standard British English in the intonation of vowel sounds, particularly in closing diphthongs (any pair of different vowels is called a diphthong). For example, *today* sounds like "todie," *high* sounds like "hoi," *hello* sounds like "helleouw," and *trout* sounds like "treout." Another common trait is the centralized "i," producing "ut" for *it* and "paintud" for *painted*. Since the early 1960s the distinction of vowel sounds in words like *ear* and *air*, *here* and *hair*, and *beer* and *bare* have become less pronounced.

PECULIARITIES

There are many compounded words, new meanings, and colloquial expressions in the language that derive from a specifically New Zealand experience and environment. Examples are *cow-cockie* (dairy farmer), *section* (plot of land), and *up the boohai* (a *boohai* is a remote district or area; *up the boohai* means "very much awry").

A NEW ZEALAND GLOSSARY

arvo	afternoon
backbone of the country	the farming community
baths	swimming pool, often referred to as "municipal baths"
beaut	something or someone of excellent quality
boozer	a public bar
chocker	filled to capacity
clobbering machine	pressure by fellow New Zealanders not to be seen as too successful
cobber	a mate (friend)
dinky-die	truly, absolutely ("I did win the game, dinky-die!")
footie	rugby union (an outdoor sport played with an oval ball by two teams of 15 players each) or league football
gidday	a common greeting
good on you	a term of encouragement
hard case	an entertaining or self-reliant person
hooray	a Kiwi farewell
joker	a bloke (Kiwi man)
kia ora (kev-ah aw-rah)	good luck (a Maori greeting)
Kiwi	a New Zealander (after the native bird)
mainland	the South Island
mate	a friend, but also used as an informal (and presumptuous) greeting to a visitor
mingie	stingy ("Don't be mingie!")
ordinary bloke, ordinary joker	a sensible Kiwi male with a humble opinion of himself
shout	to treat ("I'll shout you a meal")
sport	a way of addressing someone ("Howya, sport?")
throw a wobbly	an overdisplay of emotion, usually anger
within coo-ee of	"not to come within coo-ee of" means to fall grossly short of reaching a goal
wop-wops	"he lives in the wop-wops" means he lives in a very remote area

A class of children learning the Maori language at the predominantly Maori village of Waima.

MAORI LANGUAGE

New Zealand Maori is a Polynesian language closely related to Cook Islands Maori, Tahitian, and Hawaiian. It is the first language of some 50,000 adult Maori New Zealanders (12 percent of the Maori population). One of the most important aspects of the Maori renaissance of the 1970s was the renewal of interest among the Maori in their indigenous language. There are more speakers of Maori now than there were at the beginning of the 20th century.

Use of the Maori language was encouraged through a Maori-language preschool movement and by Maori-language immersion primary schools. The former is a *whanau*, or extended family base, where very young children are taught traditional knowledge, crafts, and customs through the medium of the Maori language. Maori-language immersion primary schools teach pupils the entire school curriculum in Maori. Thousands of secondary school pupils also take Maori language as a subject. A Maori Language Commission assists government departments and other crown agencies in offering a range of services in Maori.

MISSIONARIES BRING LITERACY

When the first missionaries arrived in New Zealand, the Maori did not have a written form of language. Their genealogies were recorded in stylized figures carved on the wooden poles of their ancestral meetinghouses, while folk art related their myths and legends. Then, in 1820, two Anglican missionaries traveled back to England, taking with them two important Maori chiefs. At Cambridge University in England they produced the first Maori grammar.

This important work was further developed during the next decade by the missionaries. The Maori people were so eager to learn that they would use gunpowder instead of chalk when the latter was not available to them. By the mid-1830s Maori who wished to be held in high regard recognized the need to be literate.

A Maori epitaph on a tombstone. By the 1840s, there were proportionately more Maori who were literate in Maori than English people literate in English. All that has, of course, changed in this day and age.

Choral notes in Maori. A survey disclosed that almost 60 percent of all schoolchildren in New Zealand, Maori and non-Maori, now study the language.

A LIVING LANGUAGE

Language is always changing, and the Maori were quick to extend their vocabulary to take foreign ideas and objects into account. Maori people began to fit foreign words to their own phonology. For example, *Hune* (HOO-ne) means "June," *moni* (mor-nee) means "money," and *hipi* (hip-ee) means "sheep."

Today Maori speakers like to adapt Maori words and phrases to express new ideas and objects. Maori vocabulary has also found its way into New Zealand English. Most of these borrowed words are proper nouns—for example, bird names such as *kiwi* and *kakapo*, plant names such as *manuka* and *kumara*, and trees such as *kauri* and *rimu*. Other Maori words add a richness of expression, such as *mana*—used to connote a person's prestige, status, or honor. *Mana* is a very important concept in Maoridom.

There are very many places in New Zealand with Maori names, including mountains, rivers, and lakes. Some of these have an English name as well. For example, Mount Taranaki is also called Mount Egmont. In tourist centers such as Rotorua and Queenstown, public information signs are displayed in several languages.

MAORI PRONUNCIATION

Every syllable in Maori should be pronounced clearly and must end with a vowel. Practice sounding the syllables separately at first, then run them together. For example, say "Maa-or-ri" for *Maori*. There are five vowel sounds, each of which may be said either short or long. The vowels sound like the following:

short a, like u in *hut*

long aa, like a in *Chicago*

short i, like i in *hit*

long ii, like ee in *keep*

short e, like e in *fleck*

long ee, like ai in *fair*

short o, like or in *distort*

long oo, like ore in *sore*

short u, like u in *put*

long uu, like oo in *spoon*

A traveler reading in an arts center bookshop in Christchurch, in the South Island of New Zealand.

Maori diphthongs retain the sound of the second vowel quite clearly, and most of them are not matched in sound by anything in English. For example, *ae* sounds like the "igh" in *high*.

Consonants are pronounced as they are in English, with the exception of *wh*, which sounds more like "f," and *ng*, which always sounds like the "ng" in the nasal-sounding *clanger* rather than *linger*.

ARTS

THROUGH THE ARTS, NEW ZEALANDERS have both sought after and found expression for their cultural identity. As they have gradually shifted their focus away from Britain and Europe for their source of cultural identity, they have begun to see themselves as part of the Asia-Pacific and an appreciation of the different colors within their own society has grown. National identity is founded less on New Zealand's being different from other countries and more on the differences found within it. Now there is one sound, but many voices.

MAORI ART

Art in New Zealand had its origins in Maori culture centuries before European settlement. While the men carved complex images out of wood, stone, and bone, the women crafted flax fiber into clothing, mats, and baskets.

Maori women were taught the ritualistic art of weaving. They mainly wove cloaks (loose outer garments): feather-decorated cloaks for mourning, ceremonial dog-skin cloaks, and closely woven cloaks designed to ward off spears in battle.

Left: **A Maori-design fence in Rotorua.**

Opposite: **The famous Christchurch Art Gallery boasts a range of curved metal sculptures, making it an interesting sight to behold.**

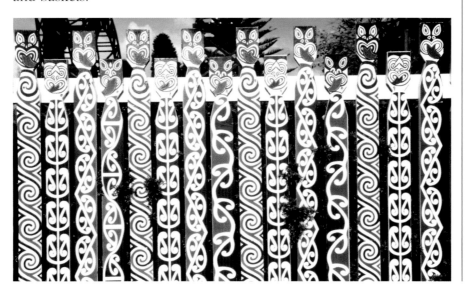

An intricately carved storehouse at the Maori Arts and Crafts Institute in Rotorua.

Carvers, trained in their youth by pre-European experts, were given high status in traditional Maori culture. The carvings usually symbolized the veneration of ancestors and appeared not only in ancestral meetinghouses but also their storehouses and war canoes. Characteristic motifs incorporated in carvings were the single and double spiral. On ceremonial occasions and in times of war, warriors painted colorful patterns on their faces and bodies. Coloring materials (usually mixed with shark oil) included white clay, charcoal, and red ocher. Red was regarded as a sacred color.

Tattooing of the body was a ritualized art that was also performed by priestly experts. Spiraled designs were incised with bone and jade chisels tapped with a rod, and colored with blue pigment. Each person's *moko* (mor-kor), or tattoo, was different and was used as a form of identification. The performing priest's own body was considered too sacred to tattoo. Instead his body designs were painted with colors derived from plants and ocher. Today tattoos are still done by experts, but using modern equipment.

EUROPEAN ART

The first European style of art in New Zealand was the pen drawings that recorded the impressions of the country created by the draftsmen who accompanied European exploratory expeditions. Then came visiting artists from Europe who were eager to paint Maori activities and artifacts, followed by British artists in the early colonial period who painted to promote the country back home in England.

Charles Goldie (1870–1947), one of New Zealand's best-known artists, is famous for his Maori portraits. Painting in the early years of the 20th century, at a time when the Maori population was thought to be dying out, his detailed portraits are of considerable historical interest and are highly valued.

In the paintings of early-19th-century artists, nature was portrayed as an overwhelming, dominant force. But as the land was cleared and cultivated by the early colonists, landscapes began to take on a different aspect. Frances Hodgkins is New Zealand's most internationally celebrated painter, known for her still-life and landscape paintings. However, much of her painting was done in England, where she spent most of her life in the early part of the 20th century.

Rita Angus (1908–70) helped give New Zealand painting a sense of its own direction during the 1930s and 1940s. Her landscapes captured the distinctive color of New Zealand with its sharp light. Colin John McCahon (1919–87) is the most important contemporary artist. He integrated spiritual words and phrases into his landscape paintings in the 1970s and 1980s, with powerful effect.

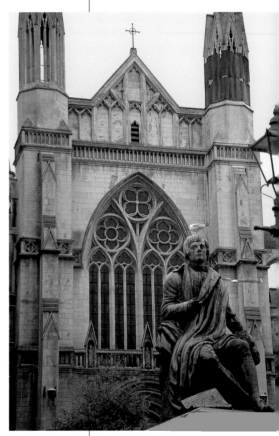

A church in Dunedin shows 19th-century architecture. A distinct New Zealand style in architecture, sculpture, pottery, and wood turning, based on a blend of European, Maori, and Asia-Pacific themes and influences, has since developed.

101

LITERATURE

Women in New Zealand have been closely involved with the arts since colonial times. In contrast with other professions, literature and the arts are more loosely structured, giving women the freedom to attain higher prominence and success.

Katherine Mansfield (1888–1923) was a prominent New Zealand modernist writer of short fiction. Born in Wellington, her original name was Kathleen Mansfield Beauchamp. She went to London at the age of 14 to finish her education and then returned to New Zealand for two years. At age 19 she went back to London, where she associated with innovative writers, such as Virginia Woolf, T. S. Eliot, and D. H. Lawrence.

Although she spent her short adult life in Europe (she died at the age of 34 from tuberculosis), many of Mansfield's stories draw on her memory of her New Zealand childhood. Her short stories, such as "Prelude" (published in 1918), "At the Bay," "The Garden Party," and many others, have earned her a reputation as one of the finest short-story writers in the English language. D. H. Lawrence compared her to Charles Dickens. Her writing is considered to be both poetic and powerful.

Katherine Mansfield. Virginia Woolf once said of her: "I was jealous of her writing. The only writing I have ever been jealous of."

Another writer, Dame Ngaio Marsh (1899–1982), became an internationally known writer of detective stories, completing more than 30 "whodunits" (stories about a crime).

New Zealand's most gifted novelist, Janet Paterson Frame (1924–2004), came to be recognized internationally in 1957 with the publication of *Owls Do Cry*. Her autobiographical trilogy—*To the Island* (1983), *An Angel at My Table* (1984), and *The Envoy from Mirror City* (1985)—was later published in one volume as *An Angel at My Table*, and an acclaimed television film was made under this title by New Zealand director Jane Campion.

Keri Hulme (born in 1947) is a novelist, short-story writer, and poet with Maori origins. She won the prestigious Booker McConnell Prize for fiction in 1985 for her novel *Bone People* (1983). Interestingly her novel, steeped in Maori mythology, was first produced in book form by a Maori women's collective and became a New Zealand bestseller through word of mouth. Subsequently an international publisher ensured a worldwide audience.

Some contemporary New Zealand writers of adult fiction have also written for children. They include Joy Cowley, Patricia Grace, and Maurice Gee. In earlier years young people growing up in New Zealand read stories and fairy tales from British and European cultures. Now these and other authors have given New Zealand children stories set in their own culture to which they can relate. Margaret Mahy is New Zealand's best-known writer for children. She has twice won the Carnegie Medal (the top international award for children's literature) for her works *The Haunting* and *The Changeover*.

James K. Baxter (1926–72) is widely regarded as the most gifted poet New Zealand has produced. He had no regard for materialistic values, and in the 1960s, he became a controversial figure, setting up a center for drug addicts founded on the same principles as Alcoholics Anonymous (an international organization that provides support for people who are trying to overcome alcoholism). His verse is considered both profound and beautiful.

The National Orchestra playing in Wellington.

MUSIC

There is a strong tradition of music in New Zealand—especially choral singing, which has been enriched by the singing traditions of the Maori and Pacific Islanders. At a local level many people love to perform in musicals, choirs, orchestras, ensembles, and bands of all kinds, including brass bands and Scottish pipe bands.

The New Zealand Symphony Orchestra (NZSO), based in Auckland and Wellington, spends much of its time traveling throughout the country, making the music of international and national composers accessible to everyone. It regularly attracts world-famous soloists and conductors and makes recordings for several major international labels. In addition to the national orchestra, there are prominent regional orchestras, a highly acclaimed New Zealand Chamber Orchestra, and a national brass band.

DOUGLAS LILBURN

Douglas Gordon Lilburn (1915–2001) was a prolific contemporary composer. His published and recorded works include symphonies, songs, and piano and guitar pieces. Eager to present a distinctive New Zealand voice, Lilburn drew inspiration from the natural environment: the light, sounds, colors, and shapes that make up New Zealand's landscapes and seascapes. This is reflected in some of the names of his compositions—for example, "Aotearoa," "Landfall in Unknown Seas," "A Song of Islands," and "Soundscape with Lake and River" (the latter is an electronic work—that is, electroacoustic music was used rather than conventional instruments). One of his best-known works is the song cycle "Sings Harry," set to Dennis Glover's poem about a romantic and tough back-country character. By his example as a composer and through his musical teachings, Lilburn has encouraged young composers to create a music tradition of their own.

MAORI SONG AND DANCE

The traditional Maori song of welcome, the *waiata*, is still alive today in Maoridom. But around the turn of the 20th century a new form of Maori music emerged, known as the action song. In a way the Maori action song has become the national dance of New Zealand. Maori concert groups perform action songs for tourists and also travel overseas. Sometimes these songs use melodies from other countries, such as "Blue Eyes," the waltz tune behind "E Pari Ra," a tribute and lament for the Maori soldiers of World War I. A Maori woman combined action song with electroacoustic dance rhythms to create an international hit, "Poi-e."

According to Maori legend, the wide, bulging eyes seen on the carved figures inside the traditional meetinghouses represent the eyes of the owl, which is seen as a wise bird. When Rongo, the god of peace, built a sacred house of learning, an owl was buried beneath it for protection against evil. It is also said that the glaring eyes of the carved figures mimic the owl glaring at the fantail (a small native bird with a tail shaped like a fan) when it annoys him with its constant and energetic flitting. Maori performers of action songs and *haka* (huh-kuh) imitate both birds: The men do so by making their eyes look fierce during the haka and the women by swinging their *poi* (poy), or small balls on the end of a string, in movements that resemble the flight of the fantail.

The *haka* is an energetic, aggressive action song, more like a chanting war dance and traditionally performed by men. Today it is commonly used by rugby teams, notably the touring All Blacks (New Zealand's national rugby team). The All Blacks perform this dance before every game.

A Maori man performing the *haka*, a traditional war dance. Through their action song, Maori people are able to express their own unique culture.

OPERA

There are professional opera companies based in Auckland, Wellington, and Christchurch, each of which presents two or three productions a year. Internationally acclaimed opera and concert singers from New Zealand include Patrick Power, Christopher Doig, Dame Malvina Major, Patricia Payne, Heather Begg, Keith Lewis, and Donald McIntyre. However, New Zealand's most famous opera singer is Gisborne-born Kiri Te Kanawa. In 1982 she was made a Dame Commander (one of the highest ranks that entail admission into knighthood, an honor allowing the recipient to use the title "Sir" [male] or "Dame" [female] before their name) of the Order of the British Empire.

KIRI TE KANAWA

Dame Kiri Janette Te Kanawa (born in 1944) is one of the world's leading operatic sopranos. She was educated at Saint Mary's College in Auckland, where she studied singing with Sister Mary Leo (a nun of the Order of the Sisters of Mercy who developed the college's already strong musical tradition, with its orchestra, choirs, and individual tuition, and also conducted the Sisters' Choir) from 1959 to 1965, when she won the New Zealand Mobil Song Quest and the Melbourne Sun-Aria competition. The following year she was awarded an arts council scholarship to study singing in London. She soon became an international star and is now sought after by the world's leading opera companies.

Te Kanawa delighted television audiences around the world when she sang at the royal wedding of Prince Charles and Princess Diana. Although she has been based in London for the past 30 years, she periodically returns to her homeland, where she attracts very large audiences and much adulation.

MOVIES

Going to the movies is a favorite pastime of New Zealanders, and New Zealand's feature film, television, and commercial production industries are applauded worldwide.

New Zealand's best-known movie-maker is probably Peter Jackson, who directed the epic *Lord of the Rings* trilogy. He is also known for his 2005 remake of *King Kong*. As a child, Jackson was a film fan, and he cited *King Kong* as his favorite movie when he was nine. He learned about author J.R.R. Tolkien after watching the first adaptation of the *Lord of the Rings*. Earning the rights to a film adaptation of the novel in 1997, he eventually signed a deal with Miramax for a trilogy.

His panoramic filming of New Zealand as Middle Earth, the setting for the trilogy, served to catapult New Zealand's majestic scenery to the forefront of the world's attention. *Lord of the Rings* tours sprung up in New Zealand after the release of the films as tourists from around the globe converged on New Zealand to enjoy the breathtaking landscapes they had seen on the screen. The trilogy, which has been verified as the highest-grossing motion pictures of all time, won 11 Oscars and 17 Academy Awards (a record for any movie trilogy). Not surprisingly Peter Jackson has become one of New Zealand's favorite sons.

New Zealand–born director Peter Jackson holding his Academy Award.

LEISURE

SPORTS PLAY AN IMPORTANT PART IN SHAPING New Zealand's national image. Achieving against all odds, overcoming hurdles and difficulties, and facing a challenge head-on are all prized qualities, both on and off the playing field. New Zealand mountaineer, the late Sir Edmund Hillary, who, in 1953, became the first man in the world (with Sherpa Tensing Norgay) to reach the summit of Mount Everest, is a prime example of this conquering spirit.

Competitive sporting activities are part of the compulsory education system. The international caliber of New Zealand's athletes has contributed a great deal to the cultural identity of New Zealand. Government policy ensures that sports, fitness, and leisure activities are available to all who wish to participate, including people with disabilities. The Hillary Commission for Sport, Fitness, and Leisure is a public funding agency for most of New Zealand's sporting and leisure activities.

In 1958 Sir Edmund Hillary became the first man to drive overland to the South Pole. He did so in specially adapted New Zealand farm tractors. Hillary is now featured on the New Zealand five-dollar note.

Left: **A man proudly holds up his catch.**

Opposite: **Two teenage girls bungee-jumping near Taupo in New Zealand.**

Jimmy Cowan from the New Zealand All Blacks rugby team makes a dash with the ball.

COMPETITIVE SPORTS

Rugby is the national sport, with the internationally renowned All Blacks starring as a symbol of national identity. The first World Cup Rugby competition in 1987 was won by the All Blacks, who remained unbeaten for four years. The All Blacks do not derive their name from race (the team contains the best New Zealand players, regardless of ethnicity), but from the color of their uniform—a black jersey and pants.

Much effort has been made to try to keep politics out of the sporting arena. However, in 1981, an exclusively all-white Springbok team from South Africa toured New Zealand. This upset many New Zealanders and caused protests.

Cricket has been played in New Zealand for over 150 years, and is New Zealand's oldest organized sport. There are both men's and women's cricket teams. New Zealand secured its first test win against the West Indies in 1956 and its first test series (a set of test matches played between teams representing different countries for a championship), against Pakistan, in 1969. Since then New Zealand has had particular success in international one-day matches, which are very popular with television viewers. The introduction of one-day matches has resulted in greater participation in the sport; it is now New Zealand's fastest growing sport at the junior level. Sir Richard Hadlee was one of the sport's outstanding players. He retired in 1990 with the world record at the time for wickets taken in test matches—431. He was also a superb fast bowler (fast bowling is a technique of bowling in cricket) and one of the world's best all-around cricket players.

THE AMERICA'S CUP

In 1993 to 1994, New Zealand yachts won the Volvo Ocean Race (formerly the Whitbread Round the World Race, a yacht race around the world). National fervor was aroused again in 1995, when the yacht *Black Magic* (*above*), crewed by Team New Zealand (a sailing team based in Auckland that represents New Zealand), won the prestigious America's Cup and successfully defended it in 2000.

Intense international interest has been shown not only in the design and special capabilities of the yachts but also in the first real-time 3D computer animation package, designed in New Zealand to relay the 1992 America's Cup race.

International success has also been achieved in track and field athletics, netball, squash, softball, golf, equestrian events, boxing, ice racing, skiing, and water sports such as yachting, rowing, windsurfing, and swimming.

New Zealand athletes are always eager participants in both the Olympic Games and the Commonwealth Games (a multinational, multisport event). The ratio of medals won per thousand of population is often high. The 18th Commonwealth Games (2006) were held in Melbourne, Australia, and New Zealand was represented by 255 athletes competing in more than 19 disciplines. This was the largest team that New Zealand had ever sent to a Commonwealth Games. One prominent sports personality is Arthur Lydiard, a marathon runner who later trained young athletes, notably the successful New Zealand Olympic runners Peter Snell and Murray Halberg.

Dame Susan Elizabeth Anne Devoy (born in 1964), the greatest squash player New Zealand has produced, dominated the women's game internationally from the second half of the 1980s to the early 1990s. In 1984, at the age of 20, she became the youngest-ever top-ranked player in the world. She lost her world title in 1989, but beat the new world champion a few weeks later to take the English Open for the sixth successive year.

New Zealanders enjoying their run down the harbor bridge during a marathon in Auckland.

LEISURE SPORTS

Fitness is an important element of the New Zealand lifestyle, with about half the population belonging to a sports, fitness, or leisure club. It is not unusual in the cities at lunchtime to see office workers jogging around the streets, parks, and waterfronts. The most popular sports are swimming, cycling, snooker/pool, tennis, and aerobics. Golf is popular with middle-aged people, while the older age group plays bowls (a precision sport in which the goal is to roll slightly radially asymmetrical balls—called bowls—closest to a smaller white ball—called the "jack," "kitty," or "sweetie"). It is played outdoors on grass or artificial surfaces and indoors on artificial surfaces. People engage in these activities not only to keep fit and healthy but also to enjoy the company of others.

THE GREAT OUTDOORS

New Zealanders love the outdoors. They are blessed with a country that possesses great variety and natural beauty. Many people like to walk the peaceful tracks in the national parks and reserves, such as the

People in raincoats hiking up the stream along the Milford Track.

33-mile (53.5-km) Milford Track in Fjordland, where they can appreciate the native flora and fauna, experience cascading waterfalls, and listen to the songs of unusual birds. Others prefer rock climbing, mountain climbing, or mountain biking. The warm waters of the east coast of the North Island provide some of the best surf, line, and spear fishing in the world, and big-game hunting offers deer, chamois, tahr, wild pigs, goats, and wallaby.

GOING BUSH

It is possible to enjoy adventures well away from civilization in New Zealand—to be able to tramp for days in alpine isolation and rough it in the back-country bush. There are a few people who spend most of their lives tramping and camping in splendid solitude. One such person was the late Barry Crump, who now appears on one of the country's postage stamps wearing the bushman's national costume—a *swandry* (a very thick woolen checked overshirt), waterproof hat, and heavy-duty boots. Crump wrote a number of humorous novels, his best and most famous being *A Good Keen Man*.

HOLIDAYS

Going on holiday is part of the Kiwi lifestyle. Usually holidays are taken in summer, mainly in January, though many people will take winter breaks to the ski fields. Families flock to camping grounds near the sea or the lakes where they can fish, swim, water ski, canoe, or sail their yachts. Some of the faster-flowing rivers are ideal for white-water rafting, while others are great for jet boat rides. Many people stay in the family bach. The bach, or small cottage, often set in a fairly remote area and containing the barest essentials, offers relaxed and simple living.

The weekend retreat to the bach or a place in a rural area is popular with those who have demanding or very busy lives. It is a chance to explore the countryside, perhaps on horseback or in tough four-wheel-drive vehicles. The more adventurous enjoy hang gliding, parachute jumping, or deep-sea diving.

When they are not making the most of their clean, green environment, New Zealanders love to read. In fact it is estimated that they read and buy more books per head of population than any other English-speaking country.

HOMES AND GARDENS

Family life centers around the home. Houses range in style from late-19th-century cottages to very modern, individually designed homes. Regional and climatic differences influenced the way the early settlers housed themselves. Large-windowed timber houses with their open verandahs in Northland contrast with the stone buildings and their smaller windows in Southland, where the climate is much cooler.

A group of people enjoying a ride on the Shotover Jet in Queenstown, on the South Island.

Today there is more emphasis on indoor/outdoor living styles, with wide glass doors that open directly onto balconies, patios, or gardens. Apart from the comparatively few inner-city apartment blocks, each house is detached, sitting on its own land. Many have two stories, while some have their own swimming pools and tennis courts. A shift away from small houses on large plots to large houses on smaller plots is noticeable. It is still the aim of the majority of New Zealanders to own their own home. However, home ownership rates have decreased after hitting a peak in 1991. This is attributed to a number of factors, the main one being the higher cost of home ownership. About 51 percent of New Zealanders do own houses, which is fewer than in many other Western countries (70 percent for the United Kingdom, 69 percent for the United States and Canada). As a nation of "do-it-yourselfers," New Zealanders devote a lot of energy and leisure time to home improvements.

A typical New Zealand home, complete with potted plants and an outdoor area within the house.

Gardening is a favorite hobby for thousands of New Zealanders. There are cottage gardens, wild gardens, formal gardens, herb gardens, native plant gardens, exotic gardens, and specialist gardens. Flower shows and television and radio programs keep keen gardeners up-to-date with the latest techniques and hybrids.

115

FESTIVALS

NEW ZEALAND'S NATIONAL HOLIDAYS include New Year's Day, Waitangi Day, Easter, ANZAC Day, the Queen's Birthday, Labor Day, and Christmas. Waitangi Day and ANZAC Day are particularly significant, as they mark turning points in the nation's history.

But festival fun is not confined to national holidays. Throughout the year and around the country, the events calendar is crowded with a great many activities, such as country music festivals, hot-air balloon fiestas, movie festivals, air pageants, opera festivals, rock fests, jazz and blues fests, fashion competitions, spring blossom festivals, and art and craft shows.

New Zealand's wide cultural mix is celebrated in Chinese dragon boat races, Welsh choral singing festivals, Japanese festivals, Irish and Scottish cultural festivals, and Asia-Pacific and Maori performing arts festivals. Queenstown's Winter Festival is a week of entertainment and revelry.

"A new generation has to deal with difficult questions of nationhood. . . . Today we grapple with the demands of expressing that sense of shared nationhood in a manner that is fair and just...By doing so we will truly honor those who fought for peace on foreign fields in our name."

—Former Prime Minister Jim Bolger, at an ANZAC Day service in 1997

Left: **A veteran remembers his fallen colleagues on ANZAC Day.**

Opposite: **Children celebrating diversity at the International Culture Festival in Auckland.**

The Waitangi Day airplane display.

WAITANGI DAY

Every year on February 6, a celebration takes place to commemorate the signing of the Treaty of Waitangi in 1840. Maori tribal leaders and many others join the governor-general, the prime minister, and leading dignitaries in a formal ceremony on the grounds of the Treaty House at Waitangi.

It is a time for New Zealanders, in particular the Maori and Pakeha, to reflect on their past, to appreciate the progress that has been made toward the unification of the two peoples, and to consider the way to move forward in the future. Waitangi Day focuses attention on the implications of the founding document of the nation.

Over the years the government has faced numerous claims by Maori tribes. Nevertheless there is still more to be achieved, because the Maori and Waitangi Day celebrations are traditionally peppered with Maori protesters. In 1997, for the first time, the official Waitangi Day ceremony took place at the governor-general's residence in Wellington—leaving Maori protesters to themselves in Waitangi. This has led New Zealand to consider changing the public holiday from Waitangi Day to New Zealand Day, in order to shift attention away from grievances and refocus on New Zealand as a multicultural nation.

ANZAC DAY

ANZAC stands for "Australian and New Zealand Army Corps," a group that was formed during World War I. On April 25, 1915, at dawn, the ANZAC landed on the beach of Gallipoli in Turkey, which was defended by the Turks. They gallantly fought a campaign that had been planned by British politicians and led by British officers. Thousands of lives were lost, and so was the campaign.

FREYBERG—FROM DENTIST TO GENERAL AND BEYOND

A young dentist working in rural New Zealand named Bernard Freyberg joined the British Navy at the beginning of World War I. At Gallipoli he distracted the attention of the Turks from the main landing by swimming ashore to a separate beach, where he came under heavy fire. His exploits became legendary, and while serving in France, he was awarded numerous medals for courage, including the highest honor, the Victoria Cross (a military decoration awarded for valor). He was wounded nine times and finished the war as a brigadier general.

During World War II, Freyberg commanded the New Zealand troops in the Middle East (the area around the eastern Mediterranean). In 1942 he was again wounded and again decorated for bravery. After the war the by-now Lord Freyberg served as governor-general of New Zealand for six years. In Britain the queen awarded him the high honorary position of lieutenant governor of Windsor Castle.

But the courage of the ANZAC in what was an impossible situation led to a celebration of the landing after the war was over. The returned soldiers paraded through the streets of London to receive honor from the king and queen outside Buckingham Palace (the official London residence of the British monarch). It marked the beginning of a new "mateship" between the Australians and New Zealanders. Today the word *ANZAC* is often used to describe a combination of effort between the two countries.

ANZAC Day is a time for New Zealanders to remember and honor their soldiers and heroes from all wars. The day starts with parades at dawn throughout the country. Old soldiers proudly wearing their medals march behind military and other brass bands to a central point of commemoration—usually a cenotaph (a monument built to honor soldiers who died in a war) on which the names of the fallen soldiers from the area are inscribed.

The ANZAC Day parade is held in memory of New Zealand's war veterans.

Many civilians, both young and old, join them. Traditionally the ANZAC service includes a trumpet fanfare, "The Last Post." Wreaths are laid, hymns are sung, and speeches are made. A national service is held in Wellington, presided over by leading officials who represent the military, government, diplomats, and the church.

Stilt walkers performing at the International Arts Festival.

CHRISTMAS

Christmas festivities in New Zealand begin around the middle of November with colorful street parades and brightly decorated shops. Although Christmas takes place in summertime in New Zealand, Santa Claus still arrives in a reindeer-driven sleigh, warmly dressed in his Nordic costume. Little children climb onto his knee in department stores and shopping malls to request toys and presents. Many of the traditions of the Northern Hemisphere are followed, including the preparation and baking of large Christmas fruitcakes and mince pies.

Gifts are exchanged on Christmas Day, which is traditionally the time when extended families get together to celebrate the festive season. Young children get up very early to see if Santa Claus has brought all the things they asked for, in exchange for the drink and piece of cake they left out for him the night before. Carols (both traditional and contemporary, reflecting Christmas in the Pacific) are sung in the churches and outdoors by candlelight.

EASTER AND OTHER HOLIDAYS

Good Friday and Easter Monday are public holidays in New Zealand. Many Christians give up a favorite food during Lent (a period of 40 days from Ash Wednesday to Holy Saturday), which leads up to Easter, as this is a time when they remember the death of Jesus.

Special foods that are traditional at Easter include hot currant buns topped with white icing in the shape of a cross, which are symbolic of Jesus's death, and chocolate eggs, which are symbolic of new life and Jesus's resurrection. Easter is also a time for special events, such as fairs, craft shows, car rallies, and club activities.

SAMUEL DUNCAN PARNELL'S EIGHT-HOUR DAY

Samuel Duncan Parnell was an English settler determined to promote working conditions in New Zealand that were far better than those in his homeland. Soon after his arrival in New Zealand, he was asked to build a store for a shipping agent. He agreed to do so on the condition that he worked only eight hours every day, arguing that there are "twenty-four hours per day given us; eight of these should be for work, eight for sleep, and the remaining eight for recreation." Because tradesmen were scarce in the new settlement, the shipping agent agreed to Parnell's terms. And so, Parnell wrote later, "the first strike for eight hours a day the world has ever seen was settled on the spot." Other employers tried to impose the traditional long hours, but Parnell met incoming ships, talked to the workmen, and enlisted their support. They agreed that anyone who broke the eight-hour rule would be dunked in the harbor. Eventually the eight-hour workday became established.

LABOR DAY This holiday was introduced in 1899 to commemorate the eight-hour work day. It falls on the fourth Monday of each October.

QUEEN'S BIRTHDAY A public holiday is celebrated on the first Monday in June to mark Queen Elizabeth II's birthday, which is actually in April. Usually the only "celebration" involves the firing of 21 cannon balls as a salute to the queen.

NEW YEAR'S DAY This holiday is really celebrated in style on New Year's Eve—leaving many people unable to celebrate the following day because they are hungover from the previous day's celebrations, which usually includes drinking.

Each province also has its own anniversary day to mark its beginnings. From time to time important events are reenacted in period costume, such as the landing of the early settlers on the beaches of the capital city.

INTERNATIONAL ARTS FESTIVAL

Every two years an arts festival is staged in Wellington, which attracts high-caliber international artists and visitors from around the globe. For over three weeks people can immerse themselves in every kind of artistic activity, from large-scale opera to mime and street art. In 2006 there were more than 400 performances involving 2,000 artists.

The 10-day Goldfields Heritage Celebrations, held every November in Otago, is an exciting affair. A horse-drawn gold coach travels the route of the old gold diggers, with each town visited holding its own celebrations.

FOOD

THE ARRIVAL OF IMMIGRANTS from Europe and the Middle East, and in particular from Asia and other parts of the Pacific, has altered the way New Zealanders think about food. New and creative ways of food preparation and presentation have evolved from a blend of ethnic influences to produce what is now described as "Pacific Rim cuisine." Nonetheless some of the traditional foods of the Maori have retained special meaning. For example, only the women of a certain tribe are allowed to eat the meat of the *kereru* (ke-re-ROO), or wood pigeon.

Above: **Both shoppers and vendors crowd the Polynesian, or "Poly" Market in Wellington.**

Opposite: **Freshly made garlic bread, pizza, salad, and wine complete this meal for a woman and her companion.**

New Zealand is blessed with an abundance of meat, seafood, fruits, and vegetables. Its people take a real interest in food and wine, and throughout the year festivals are held to promote and enjoy the food produced in different regions. For example, the second Saturday in February is the time for the Wine and Food Festival in Marlborough (the northern region of the South Island).

Marlborough is not only New Zealand's premier wine-producing district. It is also a gourmet's paradise because of the very diverse range of food produced there. In Marlborough the sounds (a long passage of water connecting two larger bodies of water or separating a mainland and an island) yield tasty salmon, greenshell mussels, snapper, tarakihi, and blue cod. The coast delivers up succulent crayfish, and the clear lakes and rivers contain excellent rainbow and brown trout. Nearby the farms produce venison and lamb, and crops of olives, hazelnuts, and wasabi grow alongside cherries, apples, berries, and garlic.

People can enjoy the local delicacies in restaurants, or they may prefer to have a picnic, which might include a slab of snapper (marinated and smoked), a chunk of fresh herb bread, some olives, sun-ripened tomatoes, and zesty pickles and wine. Picnics are a favorite way of enjoying food outdoors in summer.

GREENSHELL MUSSELS

The greenshell mussel is unique to New Zealand. This shellfish derives its name from the color of its shell. Most of the commercially exported mussels are farmed. A mussel farm consists of a series of buoys held together by long lines attached to each side of the buoy. The line is anchored to the sea floor at each end. From the long lines a series of weighed ropes hang down, but do not reach the bottom.

Fresh greenshell mussels are popular with locals.

Young mussels attach themselves to the rope and are then left to grow. After 14 to 18 months, when the mussels have reached the desired size, the rope is lifted and the mussels are harvested.

FISHING IN NEW ZEALAND

New Zealand is known as one of the greatest recreational fishing countries in the world, thanks largely to the introduction of exotic rainbow trout, brown trout, quinnat salmon, Atlantic salmon, perch, char, and a few other types of fish. The lakes and rivers of central North Island are famous for trout fishing, especially Lake Taupo and the rivers that feed it.

The rivers and lakes of the South Island are also good for trout, and the rivers of Otago and Southland have some of the best salmon fishing in the world. Saltwater fishing is also a big attraction for Kiwi anglers, especially in the warmer waters around the North Island. To conserve this magnificent resource, the New Zealand government has introduced limits on the number of finfish, rock lobster, and shellfish each person is entitled to catch in a day. Strict penalties apply for exceeding the limits.

BARBECUES

The barbecue (an outdoor meal or gathering at which meat, fish, or other foods are grilled on a rack over an open fire) is very much part of the New Zealand lifestyle. New Zealanders spend a lot of leisure time socializing, visiting friends and relatives, and sharing food. The outdoor "barbie" is a relaxed and informal way to enjoy food and company in summer, and it is usually a time when the women watch the men cook.

FISH AND CHIPS

Of all the fast foods and take-outs that are available to New Zealanders (including hamburgers and pizza), "fish and chips" is still the most popular. Introduced by the British, fish and chips consists of large portions of fish dipped in batter and french fries sprinkled with salt and vinegar. Traditionally they were always wrapped in newspaper to take out, but today more hygienic but less interesting wrapping is used.

Various species of crabs, lobsters, prawns, squid, and other shellfish are found in the oceans of New Zealand.

A Maori man cooks a traditional meal of corn, chicken, and cabbage in an earth oven.

MAORI FOOD TRADITIONS

The Maori people cooked their food in earth ovens called *hangi* (HAA-ngee). A *hangi* is prepared by digging a pit, setting up a mountainous pile of wood in it, and then placing stones on top. The fire is then lit to heat the stones.

The stones are sprinkled with water to remove ash and create steam. The food is placed on leaves on top of the stones. After several hours of slow steaming, the food is tender and very tasty. Nowadays the word *hangi* also refers to the feast itself, which always follows the main ceremony at a *marae* gathering.

LIFESTYLE FOOD

Most people in New Zealand cook with either electric or gas stoves. Kitchens are very well equipped and modern—often incorporating the latest European technology.

Family food is generally simply prepared and includes meat, fish, or poultry with potatoes, rice, or pasta, and several cooked vegetables or salads. The main course might be followed by a dessert, such as fresh fruit and ice cream. More exotic and elaborate three- or four-course meals are served for dinner parties.

The culinary high point of the week used to be the traditional, English-style roast prepared for lunch on Sundays. Although many people still like to have roast beef, lamb, or chicken occasionally, the Sunday ritual has generally been replaced by lighter food.

Despite the fact that New Zealand supermarkets are full of a large variety of fresh fruit and vegetables and scores of different cuts of meat, more and more people are buying convenience foods to keep pace with their busy lifestyles.

Eating out is hugely popular, especially with younger, working people, and lunchtime is becoming a favorite time to indulge in fine food. An interesting lunch could include a crayfish and crab apple mousse wrapped in spinach, accompanied by fresh Pacific oysters topped with salmon caviar and a New Zealand Chardonnay wine. There are numerous restaurants, particularly in the cities, where diners can choose from a wide range of cuisines, including European (French, Spanish, Greek, Italian, and Austrian), Asian (Chinese, Indian, Lebanese, Cambodian, Malay, Thai, Indonesian, and Japanese), Mexican, and, of course, New Zealand seafood. Local and national competitions encourage chefs to be innovative and reach high standards.

The ever-zesty kiwifruit is popular both locally and abroad.

KIWIFRUIT

Kiwifruit is New Zealand's leading horticultural export. It was originally known as the Chinese gooseberry because of its origins in the Yangtze Valley of China. Somehow the seeds of this subtropical plant arrived in New Zealand at the beginning of the 20th century and kiwifruit has thrived in the warmer areas of the North Island.

Over the years orchardists have found ways to improve the quality and quantity of their yield. The name was changed to kiwifruit when New Zealand started to export the fruit in the 1950s. New Zealanders like to use kiwifruit in fruit salads or as a decorative topping on a traditional dessert such as the pavlova (a sweet meringue cake).

WINE

While New Zealand shares the same latitude as the major wine-producing areas in Europe—from the Rhine Valley in the north, through Alsace, Champagne, Burgundy, Loire, and Bordeaux in France, and into southern Spain—its climatic conditions are quite different. The long, narrow shape of New Zealand's two main islands means that no location is more than 80 miles (129 km) from the sea, giving it a maritime climate.

Most of the vineyards lie in coastal areas where they bask for an average of 2,200 sunshine hours each year and are cooled at night by sea breezes. This climatic pattern provides ideal growing conditions, producing premium-quality grapes.

Wine making in New Zealand dates back to the earliest settlers. Pioneer missionary Samuel Marsden planted about 100 vines at his mission station in Kerikeri, Bay of Islands, in 1819. When James Busby, the British resident and an expert viticulturist, arrived in 1833, he set about turning Marsden's grapes into wine.

Even the French navigator Dumont d'Urville was impressed with New Zealand wine, noting in his journal, "I was given a light white wine, very sparkling and delicious in taste, which I enjoyed very much."

The French Catholic missionary Bishop Pompallier also had an interest in wine, and he established another vineyard. During the next few years, grapevines were taken to other parts of New Zealand by French missionary priests.

Hardworking immigrants from Yugoslavia and Lebanon laid the foundations of the modern New Zealand commercial wine industry early in the 20th century. But it was not until after World War II, when New Zealand servicemen returned from Europe having acquired a taste for

Local wine served with chilled glasses.

European-style table wine, that wine makers in New Zealand had a local market.

Since the 1960s there has continued to be rapid growth in wine production and consumption. Modern viticulturists have combined traditional vineyard practices with state-of-the-art techniques to enhance the flavor and produce wines with a distinctive New Zealand style. Today New Zealand wine excites the world's judges and wine media commentators. In international competitions, New Zealand regularly wins high awards for its Sauvignon Blanc, Chardonnay, Cabernet/ Merlot, and sparkling wines.

The local Speight's brewery in Dunedin.

BEER

Beer drinking, especially among New Zealand males, was very popular a long time before the now-fashionable wines appeared on the scene. Until 1967 licensing laws prohibited the sale of alcohol after 6:00 P.M. This led to frenzied drinking for 90 minutes after the factories and other workplaces closed for the day, causing what came to be known as "the six o'clock swill." Drinking hours were later extended, apparently in an effort to reduce drunkenness. Pubs can now stay open as long as they like.

The British explorer James Cook pioneered brewing in New Zealand when he established a brewery at Dusty Sound. Today there are three primary breweries. New Zealand beer is similar to English- and Netherlands-style lagers, with "Steinlager" being one of the most popular beers, both in New Zealand and abroad.

COLONIAL GOOSE

Colonial Goose is the name for a surprisingly effective preparation of roast leg of lamb. Early colonial pioneers were very inventive, as goose was very scarce in New Zealand. This dish involves carefully removing the bone from a leg of lamb, stuffing it with honey and dried apricots, and then marinating it in a red-wine-based marinade, which even gives it the appearance of goose when cooked.

You need a large leg of lamb. If you do not know how to take the bone out, ask your butcher to do it, explaining that you need to be able to stuff it.

For the stuffing
Approximately 1 ounce (30 g) butter
1 large tablespoon (15 ml) clear honey
Approximately 4.5 ounces (125 g)
  dried apricots, finely diced
1 medium-sized onion, finely diced
1 cup (110 g) fresh bread crumbs
¼ teaspoon (2 g) of salt
¼ teaspoon (½ g) of dried thyme
Freshly ground black pepper
1 beaten egg

For the marinade
9 ounces (250 g) sliced carrots
2 large onions, sliced
1 bay leaf
3 or 4 crushed parsley stalks
1 cup (250 ml) of red wine

1. To prepare the stuffing, melt the butter and honey over low heat, add the other ingredients, and combine well.
2 Force the stuffing into the cavity of the meat, and sew it up with fine string.
3. Place the leg into a plastic bag (which sits in a large bowl), and add the marinade mixture.
4. The meat is best prepared just after breakfast, so it can be regularly turned over in the marinade throughout the day.
5. Cook in oven at 350°F (180°C) for two hours, but check on its progress after 90 minutes. If the meat looks like it is overbrowning, it should be covered with foil.
6. Remove the string before carving.
7. Strain the marinade and use three or four tablespoons of the strained liquid to make gravy.

PAVLOVA

Pavlova is a meringue dessert named after the Russian ballet dancer Anna Pavlova. It is crispy on the outside but light and fluffy inside.

6 egg whites
1 teaspoon (5 ml) vanilla essence
1 teaspoon (5 ml) cider vinegar or lemon juice
7 ounces (200 g) sugar
1 dessertspoon (3 g) corn flour

1. Whisk the egg whites in a bowl until they are dry and form stiff peaks.
2. Gradually add two spoonfuls of sugar at a time while continuing to whisk. The mixture should become thick and glossy.
3. Sieve the corn flour over the egg mixture, add the vanilla and vinegar, and gently fold to combine.
4. Pile the mixture high on baking paper.
5. Bake at 250°F (125°C) for one hour. When cooked, the pavlova should be a light cream color.
6. Turn the oven off and cool the pavlova in the oven for three hours with the door closed.
7. Serve with cream and fruit of your choice.

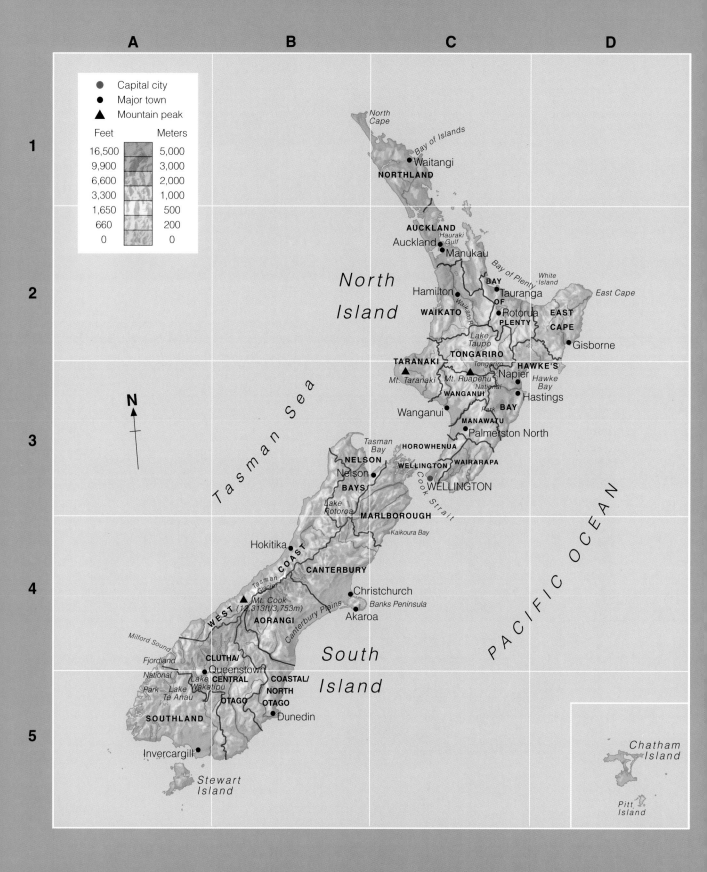

A   B   C   D

1

Capital city
Major town
Mountain peak

Feet	Meters
16,500	5,000
9,900	3,000
6,600	2,000
3,300	1,000
1,650	500
660	200
0	0

North Cape

Bay of Islands

Waitangi

NORTHLAND

AUCKLAND

Auckland

Hauraki Gulf

Manukau

Bay of Plenty

White Island

2

North Island

Hamilton

BAY OF PLENTY

Tauranga

Rotorua

WAIKATO

Waikato R.

EAST CAPE

East Cape

Gisborne

Lake Taupo

TONGARIRO

TARANAKI

Tongariro

HAWKE'S

Mt. Taranaki

Mt. Ruapehu

National

Napier

Tasman Sea

WANGANUI

Hawke Bay

Hastings

Wanganui

Park

BAY

MANAWATU

Palmerston North

N

3

HOROWHENUA

Tasman Bay

WELLINGTON

WAIRARAPA

NELSON

Nelson

Cook Strait

WELLINGTON

BAYS

Lake Rotoroa

MARLBOROUGH

Kaikoura Bay

PACIFIC OCEAN

Hokitika

WEST COAST

CANTERBURY

4

Tasman Glacier

Mt. Cook
(12,313ft/3,753m)

Christchurch

Banks Peninsula

Milford Sound

WEST

AORANGI

Canterbury Plains

Akaroa

Fjordland

South Island

National

CLUTHA/

Queenstown

Park

Lake Te Anau

Lake Wakatipu

CENTRAL

COASTAL/ NORTH OTAGO

OTAGO

SOUTHLAND

Dunedin

5

Invercargill

Stewart Island

Chatham Island

Pitt Island

MAP OF NEW ZEALAND

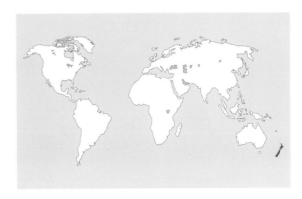

ECONOMIC NEW ZEALAND

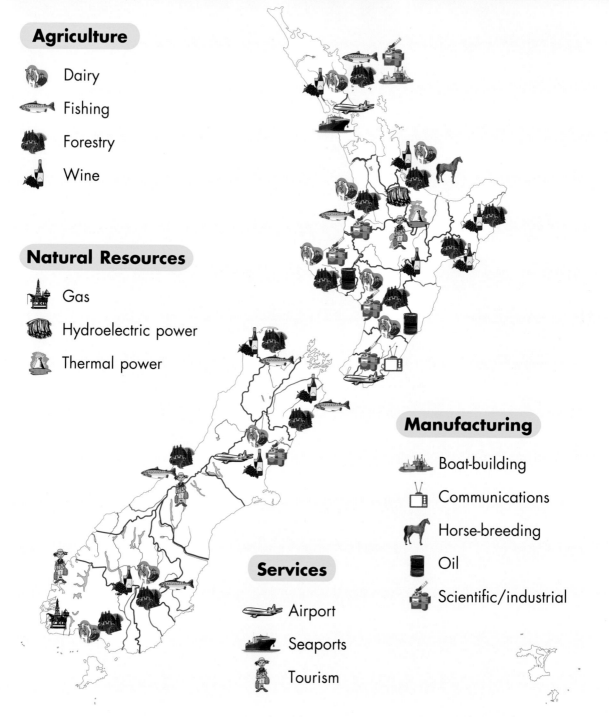

Agriculture
- Dairy
- Fishing
- Forestry
- Wine

Natural Resources
- Gas
- Hydroelectric power
- Thermal power

Manufacturing
- Boat-building
- Communications
- Horse-breeding
- Oil
- Scientific/industrial

Services
- Airport
- Seaports
- Tourism

ABOUT THE ECONOMY

OVERVIEW
The economy of New Zealand is a market economy that is greatly dependent on international trade. Tourism has overtaken agriculture as the main source of foreign exchange. Agriculture and manufacturing remain the pillars of the economy, and there is a fledgling film industry. Economic free-market reforms over the last decades have removed many barriers to foreign investment, and the World Bank has praised New Zealand as the most business-friendly country in the world. New Zealand welcomes foreign investment without discrimination, but groups such as Campaign Against Foreign Control of Aotearoa (CAFCA) protest the fact that New Zealand's economy is now substantially owned by overseas interests. New Zealand has free trade agreements with Australia, Brunei, Chile, and Singapore, and seeks other free trade agreements in the Pacific area.

GROSS DOMESTIC PRODUCT (GDP)
112.6 billion (in U.S. dollars) (2007 estimate)

GDP GROWTH
3 percent (2007 estimate)

LAND USE
Arable land 5.54 percent; permanent crops 6.92 percent; others 87.54 percent (2005 estimates)

CURRENCY
New Zealand dollar (NZD)
Notes: $5, $10, $20, $50, $100
Coins: 10 cents, 20 cents, 50 cents, $1, $2
1 USD=1.38 NZD (December 2007)

NATURAL RESOURCES
Hydropower, coal, natural gas, oil, iron ore, sand, timber, gold, limestone

AGRICULTURAL PRODUCTS
Dairy products, forest products, fruit, fish, meat, and crops

MAJOR EXPORTS
Dairy products, meat, wood and wood products, fish, machinery, and meat

MAJOR IMPORTS
Oil, vehicles, machinery, electrical equipment, iron, and steel

MAIN TRADE PARTNERS
Australia, United States, Japan, China, United Kingdom, Korea, Germany, and Singapore

WORKFORCE
2.23 million (2007 estimate)

UNEMPLOYMENT RATE
3.5 percent (2007 estimate)

INFLATION
2.5 percent (2007 estimate)

EXTERNAL DEBT
$50.02 billion (2007 estimate)

CULTURAL NEW ZEALAND

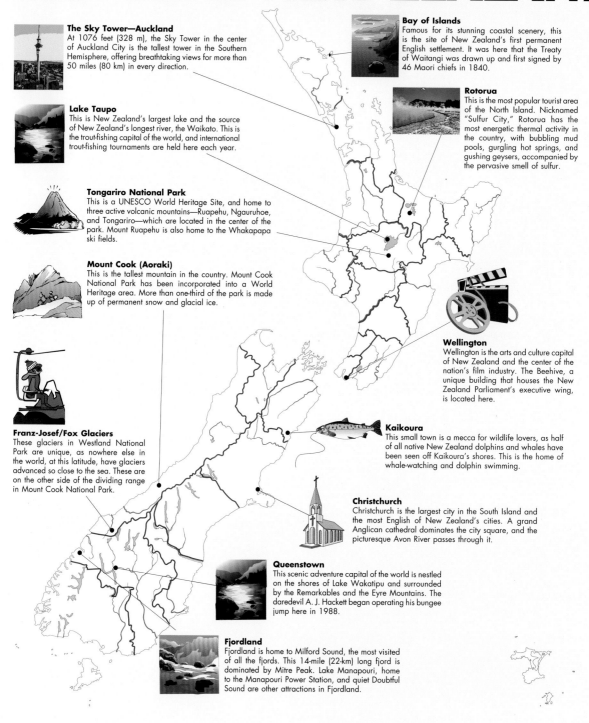

The Sky Tower—Auckland
At 1076 feet (328 m), the Sky Tower in the center of Auckland City is the tallest tower in the Southern Hemisphere, offering breathtaking views for more than 50 miles (80 km) in every direction.

Lake Taupo
This is New Zealand's largest lake and the source of New Zealand's longest river, the Waikato. This is the trout-fishing capital of the world, and international trout-fishing tournaments are held here each year.

Tongariro National Park
This is a UNESCO World Heritage Site, and home to three active volcanic mountains—Ruapehu, Ngauruhoe, and Tongariro—which are located in the center of the park. Mount Ruapehu is also home to the Whakapapa ski fields.

Mount Cook (Aoraki)
This is the tallest mountain in the country. Mount Cook National Park has been incorporated into a World Heritage area. More than one-third of the park is made up of permanent snow and glacial ice.

Franz-Josef/Fox Glaciers
These glaciers in Westland National Park are unique, as nowhere else in the world, at this latitude, have glaciers advanced so close to the sea. These are on the other side of the dividing range in Mount Cook National Park.

Bay of Islands
Famous for its stunning coastal scenery, this is the site of New Zealand's first permanent English settlement. It was here that the Treaty of Waitangi was drawn up and first signed by 46 Maori chiefs in 1840.

Rotorua
This is the most popular tourist area of the North Island. Nicknamed "Sulfur City," Rotorua has the most energetic thermal activity in the country, with bubbling mud pools, gurgling hot springs, and gushing geysers, accompanied by the pervasive smell of sulfur.

Wellington
Wellington is the arts and culture capital of New Zealand and the center of the nation's film industry. The Beehive, a unique building that houses the New Zealand Parliament's executive wing, is located here.

Kaikoura
This small town is a mecca for wildlife lovers, as half of all native New Zealand dolphins and whales have been seen off Kaikoura's shores. This is the home of whale-watching and dolphin swimming.

Christchurch
Christchurch is the largest city in the South Island and the most English of New Zealand's cities. A grand Anglican cathedral dominates the city square, and the picturesque Avon River passes through it.

Queenstown
This scenic adventure capital of the world is nestled on the shores of Lake Wakatipu and surrounded by the Remarkables and the Eyre Mountains. The daredevil A. J. Hackett began operating his bungee jump here in 1988.

Fjordland
Fjordland is home to Milford Sound, the most visited of all the fjords. This 14-mile (22-km) long fjord is dominated by Mitre Peak. Lake Manapouri, home to the Manapouri Power Station, and quiet Doubtful Sound are other attractions in Fjordland.

ABOUT THE CULTURE

OFFICIAL NAME
New Zealand

FLAG DESCRIPTION
The New Zealand flag features, on a royal blue background, a Union Jack in the first quarter and four five-pointed red stars of the Southern Cross on the fly. The stars have white borders.

TOTAL AREA
103,738 square miles (268,680 square km)

CAPITAL
Wellington

ETHNIC GROUPS
European and New Zealander 71 percent, Maori 13 percent, Asian 8 percent, Pacific Islander 6 percent, others 2 percent (2006 estimates)

RELIGION
Christianity (56 percent): Anglican 15 percent, Roman Catholic 12 percent, Presbyterian 11 percent, Methodist 3 percent, Pentecostal 2 percent, Baptist 1 percent, other Christian denominations 12 percent
Free thinkers (35 percent)
Other religions (9 percent)

BIRTHRATE
13.61 births per 1,000 New Zealanders (2007 estimate)

DEATH RATE
7.54 deaths per 1,000 New Zealanders (2007 estimate)

AGE STRUCTURE
0 to 14 years: 20.8 percent
15 to 64 years: 67.3 percent
65 years and over: 11.9 percent (2007 estimates)

MAIN LANGUAGES
English (official), Maori (official), New Zealand Sign Language (official)

LITERACY
People age 15 and over who can both read and write: 99 percent (2006 estimate)

LEADERS IN POLITICS
David Russell Lange—prime minister (July 26, 1984, to August 8, 1989)
Geoffrey Winston Russell Palmer—prime minister (August 9, 1989, to September 4, 1990)
Michael (Mike) Kenneth Moore—prime minister (September 5, 1990, to October 27, 1990)
James (Jim) Brendan Bolger—prime minister (October 28, 1990, to December 8, 1997)
Jennifer (Jenny) Mary Shipley—prime minister (December 9, 1997, to December 10, 1999)
Helen Elizabeth Clark—prime minister (December 10, 1999, to present)

TIME LINE

IN NEW ZEALAND	IN THE WORLD

circa A.D. 1000
Maori ancestors arrive at New Zealand on seven legendary canoes from Hawaiki, the mother island of the east Polynesians.

A.D. 1206–1368
Genghis Khan unifies the Mongols and starts conquest of the world. At its height, the Mongol Empire under Kublai Khan stretches from China to Persia and parts of Europe and Russia.

1769
British Captain James Cook explores the coasts of both the North and the South islands of New Zealand, also in 1773 and 1777.

1815
The first British missionaries arrive.

1840
Treaty of Waitangi between British and several Maori tribes pledge protection of Maori land and establishes British law in New Zealand.

1845 to 1872
The New Zealand Wars, also referred to as the Land Wars, occur. Maori put up resistance to British colonial rule.

1893
New Zealand becomes the world's first nation to grant women the right to vote.

1907
New Zealand becomes a dominion within the British Empire.

1914
Outbreak of World War I; New Zealand commits thousands of troops to the British war effort.

1914
World War I begins.

1915
New Zealand suffers heavy casualties in the Gallipoli campaign in Turkey.

1939
World War II begins.

1939–1945
Troops from New Zealand see action in Europe, North Africa, and the Pacific during World War II.

1945
The United States drops atomic bombs on Hiroshima and Nagasaki.

1947
New Zealand gains full independence from Britain.

1949
The North Atlantic Treaty Organization (NATO) is formed.

1984
Labour Party government elected; Prime Minister David Lange begins radical economic reforms.

1985
New Zealand refuses to allow U.S. nuclear-powered or nuclear-armed ships to enter its ports. French secret service agents blow up Greenpeace ship *Rainbow Warrior* in Auckland Harbor.

1986
Nuclear power disaster at Chernobyl in Ukraine

IN NEW ZEALAND	IN THE WORLD
1989 Prime Minister Lange resigns, replaced by Geoffrey Palmer.	
1990 Palmer resigns just before the general election, which is won by the opposition National Party. James Bolger becomes prime minister.	**1991** Breakup of the Soviet Union
1993 National Party narrowly wins election; referendum introduces proportional representation.	
1996 Under new electoral system, number of Maori MPs rises from six to 15.	
1997 After leadership challenge, Bolger resigns and Jenny Shipley becomes New Zealand's first female prime minister.	**1997** Hong Kong is returned to China.
1998 Waitangi Tribunal orders government to return confiscated land in Turangi Township to its Maori owners.	
1999 The Labour Party wins election. Helen Clark becomes prime minister.	**2001** Terrorists crash planes in New York, Washington, D.C., and Pennsylvania
2002 Prime Minister Helen Clark apologizes to Samoa for New Zealand's poor treatment of its citizens during colonial times. The Labour Party's Helen Clark wins a second term in a general election.	**2003** War in Iraq begins.
2004 Intense debate over proposed bill to nationalize the sea bed. Maori protesters say that the bill would infringe on ancestral rights. Parliament passes a bill that recognizes civil unions between homosexual couples.	
2005 Incumbent Prime Minister Helen Clark secures a narrow election win over the National Party.	
2006 Queen of the indigenous Maori population, Te Arikinui Dame Te Atairangikaahu, dies at the age of 75 after a reign of 40 years.	
2008 Sir Edmund Hillary, one of the first climbers of Mount Everest and explorers of the South Pole, dies at the age of 88 in Auckland.	

GLOSSARY

Aorangi (ah-or-rung-ee)
"Cloud piercer;" Maori name for Mount Cook

Aotearoa (ah-or-te-ah-roar)
"Land of the long white cloud;" Maori name for New Zealand

haka **(huh-kuh)**
Energetic, aggressive action song traditionally performed by men; commonly performed today by the national rugby team, the All Blacks, before a match

hangi **(HAA-ngee)**
Earth oven used by the Maori to cook food; today it also refers to the feast itself

hapu **(huh-POO)**
Subtribe

hui **(hoo-ee)**
Maori social and political gathering to which Europeans may be invited

iwi **(ee-wee)**
Tribe

karanga **(kah-rah-ngah)**
Call to visitors (always made by a woman) to enter the meetinghouse; the *karanga* is returned by a female leader on behalf of the visitors

kumara **(KOO-mah-rah)**
Sweet potato

mana **(mah-nah)**
Prestige, status, or honor

marae **(mah-rye)**
Social place where religious and secular activities take place; a rural Maori concept that has also been established in the cities

Mayflower
The famous ship that transported the English Separatists, better known as the Pilgrims, from Plymouth, England, to Plymouth, Massachusetts, in 1620

moko **(mor-kor)**
Tattoo; each person's tattoo was traditionally a form of identification

pa **(PAA)**
An earthwork fort commonly built by pre-European Maori

Pakeha (PAA-ke-haa)
Maori term for the European settlers in New Zealand

poi **(poy)**
Small balls on the ends of strings used by female Maori performers

pyroclastic
Rocks that are formed as a result of volcanic ash

tapu **(tuh-poo)**
Maori word associated with Maori spiritual beliefs, meaning "sacred" or "holy"

whanau **(FAA-no-oo)**
Extended family

FURTHER INFORMATION

BOOKS

Brown, Ben and Taylor, Helen. *Natural New Zealand*. Birkenhead, Auckland: Reed, 2004.

Deverson, Tony. *New Zealand Pocket Oxford Dictionary*. Melbourne, Victoria: Oxford University Press, 2003.

Di Piazza, Francesca and Dipiazza, Francesca. *New Zealand in Pictures*. Minneapolis: Lerner Publications, 2005.

Gillespie, Carol Ann. *New Zealand (Modern World Nations)*. New York: Chelsea House Publishers, 2005.

O'Brien, Gregory. *Welcome to the South Seas: Contemporary New Zealand Art for Young People*. Auckland: Auckland University Press, 2005.

Smith, Philippa Mein. *A Concise History of New Zealand*. Melbourne, Victoria: Cambridge University Press, 2005.

Torckler, Gillian and Torckler, Darryl. *Life-Size Guide to New Zealand Fish*. Glenfield, Auckland: Random House, 2003.

WEBSITES

Department of Conservation New Zealand. http://www.doc.govt.nz/

Kiwi Conservation Club. http://www.kcc.org.nz/

The Main Maori Site on the Net. http://www.maori.org.nz/

New Zealand in History. http://history-nz.org/index.html

FILMS

New Zealand to the Max. DVD. American Public Television, 2007.

The Ultimate New Zealand. DVD. Custom Flix, 2006.

MUSIC

Kiri Te Kanawa: Maori Songs. EMI Classics, 1999.

Te Runga Rawa: New Zealand: Maoris Songs. Playsound, 2007.

Various Artists: Songs of New Zealand. MasterSound, 2000.

BIBLIOGRAPHY

Bain, Carolyn and Dunford, George. *Lonely Planet New Zealand*. Oakland, CA: Lonely Planet Publications Pte Ltd, 2006.

Butler, Sue. *New Zealand—Culture Smart!: A Quick Guide to Customs and Etiquette*. New York: Kuperard, 2006.

Chesters, Graeme. *Living and Working in New Zealand, Third Edition: A Survival Handbook*. London: Survival Books Ltd, 2006.

Elder, Alexander. *Straying from the Flock: Travels in New Zealand*. Hoboken, NJ: Wiley, 2005.

Emmler, Clemens and Viedebantt, Klaus. *New Zealand: Continent in a Nutshell*. New York: Bucher, 2007.

Holden, Philip. *Station Country, Back-Country Life in New Zealand*. Auckland: Hodder & Stoughton Ltd, 1993.

Horrell, Steve. *Emigrating to New Zealand (How to)*. Oxford: How To Books, 2006.

Joyce, Ray and Saunders, Bill. *Discover New Zealand, The Glorious Islands*. Auckland: Landsdowne Press, 1982.

King, Michael. *The Penguin History of New Zealand*. Melbourne, Victoria: Penguin Books, 2003.

Masson, Jeffrey Moussaieff. *Why I Live in New Zealand*. New York: Ballantine Books, 2004.

Sinclair, Keith. *The Oxford Illustrated History of New Zealand*. Auckland: Oxford University Press, 1996.

Arts and entertainment. www.artcyclopedia.com/artists/goldie_charles.html

Asia-Pacific Economic Cooperation. http://www.apec2007.org/

The Beehive. http://www.beehive.govt.nz/

CIA—The World Factbook. http://www.cia.gov/library/publications/the-world-factbook/geos/nz.html

Cook Strait. http://www.tiscali.co.uk/reference/encyclopaedia/hutchinson/m0013602.html

Department of Conservation, New Zealand. http://www.doc.govt.nz/

Greenpeace. www.greenpeace.org/international

Inventions. www.nzedge.com/heroes/pearse.html

Market New Zealand. www.marketnewzealand.com

Ministry for the Environment, New Zealand. http://www.mfe.govt.nz/

Ministry of Agriculture and Forestry, New Zealand. www.maf.govt.nz

Ministry of Fisheries, New Zealand. http://www.fish.govt.nz/

National Climate Centre, New Zealand. http://www.niwascience.co.nz/

New Zealand government. http://www.doc.govt.nz/templates/podcover.aspx?id=33162

New Zealand on the Web. http://nzguide.newzealand.co.nz/guide/

New Zealand provinces and cities. http://www.state.gov/r/pa/ei/bgn/35852.htm

New Zealand timeline. http://timelines.ws/countries/NEWZEALAND.HTML

The New Zealand Treasury. http://www.treasury.govt.nz/New Zealand. http://en.wikipedia.org

Save the Whales. http://www.savethewhales.com/

Statistics New Zealand. http://www2.stats.govt.nz

Wellington. http://www.wellingtonnz.com/about_wellington/wellington_facts/population

INDEX